BIG MEETINGS, BIG RESULTS

BIG MEETINGS BIG RESULTS

Strategic Event Planning
for Productivity and Profit

Tom McMahon

NTC Business Books
a division of *NTC Publishing Group* • Lincolnwood, Illinois USA

Cover and text design: John Zehethofer
Cover photo: Tom Grill/Miller Comstock Inc.

This edition first published in 1990 by NTC Business Books,
a division of NTC Publishing Group,
4255 West Touhy Avenue,
Lincolnwood (Chicago), Illinois 60646-1975 U.S.A.
Copyright © 1988 by Gage Educational Publishing Company.
All rights reserved. No part of this book may
be reproduced, stored in a retrieval system, or
transmitted in any form, or by any means, electronic,
mechanical, photocopying or otherwise, without
the prior permission of NTC Publishing Group.
Manufactured in the United States of America.
Library of Congress Catalog Card Number: 89-61539

9 0 BC 9 8 7 6 5 4 3 2 1

To Arlene,
my friend and partner and inspiration.

Contents

List of Figures

ACKNOWLEDGMENTS

In writing any book, there are an almost limitless number of people an author can thank. I have tried my best to acknowledge as many of my associates, acquaintances, and friends as memory allows. If anyone has been missed, please know that I will always be grateful, even if I have neglected to name you here.

First, I want to thank Dan Stoffman, who helped me to author this work. His interest and the questions he asked were very helpful in clarifying and occasionally rectifying my own ideas. My thanks also to June Trusty, who did a thorough job in editing the book, and to Bob McElman and Joan Homewood at Gage, whose comments and suggestions helped to give the book its final shape.

Among the many professionals that I have worked with, I want to thank Mrs. Rachel King and Mr. Peter Carr-Locke for their insights. Mr. John Edward deserves special thanks for his careful reading of my manuscript and the excellent observations he provided. Mr. Dick King and Mr. John Shepherd each provided me with first class case histories and a lot of interest and support. As clients, they worked closely with me in producing many top rate events over the years.

Among my fellow consultants there are several special individuals who put many a deep and thought-provoking suggestion into my many drafts. Dr. Lance Secretan, a fellow author and international consultant, kept me thinking business and results, while Dr. Phil Johnson never let me forget about the people part of this business. Mr. Bryan Tyson helped me to remember that flair is an important ingredient in everything we do.

Finally I would like to thank my friends at TEEG, The Exceeding Expectations Group, who have worked together to produce

xiv   BIG MEETINGS — BIG RESULTS

some of the finest results-oriented business programs ever: Mr. Kevin Hood, Mr. Lou Klevinas, Mrs. Honey Sherman, Mrs. Rena Cohen, Ms. Lynn Stanley, Mr. Greg Smith, and Mr. Mike Hines. A special thanks to Mrs. Laura Miller who has demonstrated that she is without doubt the best corporate trainer in North America and who has easily doubled the results we have been able to achieve from our Big Meetings!

INTRODUCTION

Approximately $3 billion is spent every year on large business meetings in North America. Sadly, much of that money is ill-spent because those who head the organizations involved neglect to think through what they want their meetings to achieve and what message they want to present. Whether you are the chief executive officer of a business or the senior executive of a non-profit organization, the challenge you face is the same — to ensure that your organization's investment in big meetings yields big results.

The Meeting Is The Message

Large meetings such as conventions, conferences, and sales and annual meetings are part of the ongoing internal advertising campaign that successful organizations mount 365 days of the year. Like any effective advertising such a meeting has to be based on good market research, it has to be condensed, and it has to have one key message that is repeated over and over again so that it sinks into everyone's consciousness.

The person at the top of an organization has the clearest vision of where the organization is going. That makes him or her the person best qualified to define that key message. There are meeting planners, either in-house or specialists from outside, who can plan the logistical side of a meeting. But the communications side — the message in your meeting — is too important to be left to a meeting planner. If the message isn't the right one, the meeting will be a wasted opportunity.

Most meeting planners are oriented toward solving logistical problems such as travel arrangements, meeting rooms, and food.

The communications side, which addresses the vital questions of what will be said, learned, and felt at a meeting, usually takes second place. The purpose of this book is to show the senior executive of the organization how to replace that misguided emphasis with an organized, integrated, new approach that gives pride of place to content.

Of course, it's important that name tags be spelled correctly and that audio-visual equipment work perfectly. As senior executive you will delegate members of your staff to plan and coordinate the event, and several parts of this book (Chapters 9 and 10 in particular) are devoted to telling those planners and coordinators how to get the logistical details right every time. But the most important parts of this book are addressed to you, the senior executive. These sections detail the different ways in which you can determine precisely what you want to achieve at your meeting and, by employing effective follow-up methods, whether the effects last until the next meeting. While this may sound like a simple matter, it's really quite a complex process.

It's worth the effort, however, because once you understand what it is that you're trying to do, everything else falls into place. If you know what you want to achieve, you know your message. You also know who will be invited and how the material can best be presented to those particular people. Only when those issues are decided, can the logistical decisions be made. The beauty of this approach is that if the content decisions are the right ones, the logistical choices become obvious.

A case in point was the company that asked me to arrange a meeting on the occasion of its launch of an improved version of a water-softening salt. The first thing I asked senior management was, "Why do you want to hold this meeting?"

"Why, to sell as much of the new product as we possibly can," they replied.

"Oh, then you're planning to bring all your customers to the meeting?"

"Of course not. This meeting is for the salespeople."

"You mean you're trying to sell your salespeople on this new product?"

Well, yes, when they thought about it, that's exactly what they were trying to do, because the salespeople weren't happy. They had been selling the old version of the product successfully for twenty years.

So the real purpose of this meeting was to give the salespeople a satisfying answer to the old question, "If it ain't broke, why fix it?" The salespeople needed an answer to that question because salespeople don't deal in product development; they deal in sales per day or per client. Knowing exactly what the company needed to achieve in that meeting determined what the theme of the meeting would be and who would address that theme.

The original theme — "Let's Sell As Much of This New Product As We Can" — now became "The Best Just Got Better." Together with the company's senior management, I developed an analogy with athletes who are always striving to better their best records. Even world champion record holders try to do this — and they often succeed.

We cancelled the original plan to have corporate executives give the salespeople a pep talk. Instead, we flew in a salesman from the parent company in the United States, where the product had already been introduced. He brought the issue to life for the Canadian salespeople in a way the senior management couldn't have. He explained that, yes, the best had gotten better: the new water-softening salt was easy to sell and customers were responding well to it.

Instead of *saying* that the product was an improvement, the company *proved* that fact to its salespeople. As a result, more significant change took place for those salespeople in a half day than had taken place in the previous twelve months. And the new product subsequently sold like gangbusters.

The success of this meeting originated at the very top. The person ultimately responsible for steering the company in the marketplace had to take the initiative. He had to examine some fundamentals in a way never done before. He responded to such questions as

"Exactly what business are you in?"

"Why do you want to hold this meeting?"

"How well do you understand your people?"

"What eventual results, specifically, do you want to see?"

"What is the real operating philosophy of your company?"

It was tough for the vice presidents to examine some basic facts about themselves. It was even tougher for the president to acknowledge areas of needed improvement. All of these executives were eager to delegate full responsibility for the meeting to a subordinate. It was only because they were persuaded otherwise that the meeting was a success.

The Wrong Approach: Presto!

Zeroing in on the nuances of theme and content is crucial to a meeting's success. Yet it happens only rarely, because most meeting planners are not the leaders of the organization. They are usually junior people who are preoccupied with a logistical approach that says, in effect, "I don't know exactly what we're going to do when we get there, but let's just find the spot."

This attitude is a carryover from a time when the logistical problems of holding a meeting often were all but insurmountable. Twenty years ago, there were few convention centers, and only a handful of hotels had adequate meeting facilities. The result was a lot of pressure on the planner to find a site quickly, particularly since the habit then was to arrange meetings at the last minute. This combination of a shortage of time plus a shortage of space created pressure that led inevitably to a logistical approach.

The other response was the use of a big gimmick to cover up the failure to plan. Many intelligent executives bought into this "showbiz" approach. After all, Marshall McLuhan had told us that the medium was the message, and management, pressed for solutions to complex problems, took McLuhan literally to mean that hoopla and hype could replace content. Theatricals, chorus lines, and big-band music overwhelmed any message that senior executives might have wanted to convey. People often had a great time at these meetings but they were not undergoing any significant change.

A logistical meeting planner to whom a meeting is delegated deals with travel agents, hotels, guest speakers, and audio-visual houses. The planner takes all these elements, puts them into a box, gives the box a good shake, dumps it out — and presto! Magically, it all fits together and you have a meeting. The problem is, you don't necessarily have a successful meeting because the elements may not be the right ones and they may not be in the right combination for the results you are seeking.

The Right Approach: Mounting a Production

For the communications-oriented executive, a meeting isn't a box to be shaken, it isn't a series of checklists, it isn't a lot of hype. Instead, it is a creative act, comparable to making a movie or mounting a stage play.

Think about the last time you watched a play or movie that you thoroughly enjoyed. Did you stop to ask yourself what it was that so enthralled you? Certainly there must have been a lot of creativity, ingenuity, and screen or stage "magic" involved. But behind it all there probably was a solid, appealing story that you could relate to as a person. That story started as a concept based on a single, powerful idea. There was a fundamental focus that held your attention until the story was resolved. Your imagination and emotions were stimulated and drawn into what was unfolding on the screen or stage.

A meeting also needs a strong "story" to tell. Like a play or movie, a meeting is larger than life because, while everyday life goes on 24 hours a day, 365 days a year, a meeting is a special event, lasting only a short time. That's why your meeting must be tightly scripted to communicate its one key message with a maximum of emotional impact.

The ability to drive home one message without boring an audience to death is what separates the amateurs from the professionals. It can only be achieved — on a Broadway stage or in a meeting room — by careful preparation. Although planning the typical meeting for two hundred people is an enterprise that usually takes at least six months, your key role need take only a few hours. That is because this planning process should take place in the context of your organization's long-term strategy — of which *you* have the most in-depth knowledge. While special, a meeting is not separate from the rest of the organization's existence. To achieve outstanding results from your meeting, you should say to yourself, "This organization is going to become even better, and this meeting is one step in that becoming."

Thinking Big

Making your meeting an integral part of your long-term organization plan will produce both immediate and long-term results. For example, I recently completed a major event for one of the world's largest franchise organizations. The president, a far-sighted and sensitive individual, had the idea that a conference could play a key role in his plans to begin changing his company.

After giving it much thought, he decided that his corporation needed significant upgrading and modernization at four key levels: product range, delivery systems and facilities, manufacturing and marketing. The significant changes that he was envisioning for each segment would have a profound effect on the revenue and profit mix. He therefore felt that the way these changes were introduced could help to determine levels of acceptance and long-term commitment. He was insightful enough to realize that an effective "sell" up front could be leveraged over the long run and act as a focus for future developments.

On a measurable level he was asking for an investment from each franchisee equivalent to a little less than a year's gross revenue. He was projecting a three-year increase in top-line sales of at least fifty percent. He was also projecting privately another ten- to twenty-five percent yearly incremental volume growth. If the franchisees refused to go along with these changes they stood to lose up to fifteen percent in sales in a stiffer, competitive market.

To save time and guarantee the end result, he chose to work with us on a meeting that used a three-part strategy to

1. convince the participants that it was time for a change of this sort
2. demonstrate that everything was in place to bring about this change quickly and efficiently
3. guarantee the participants that whatever changes they made would be supported 110 percent by the corporation.

This meeting strategy, which was identical to his overall business strategy, not only worked but provided an extra benefit: several franchisees decided to turn control of their outlets over to the parent body because they knew that they couldn't stay around for the long run. This increased the company's leverage position and is helping to ensure long-term success. The president also guaranteed his program's success by developing a strong follow-up campaign based on the meeting's content and thrust. The original investment in the planning and production of the meeting itself has already shown a fourfold payback in terms of sales from one region alone!

Not every meeting will produce such dramatic gains, but all well-planned meetings have measurable, positive results. This book will help you to understand the dynamics of effectively lining up the dominoes to create the right infrastructure to achieve success. Since you are responsible for all of the results that your organization attains, you should be the one to knock over that first domino.

The challenge I present to you, then, is to become the executive director of this important production — your organization's meeting. A creative executive director has a quality of mind that I call "expansiveness." This means being able to break out of old molds and adopt new ways of thinking and new ways of doing things. It means having a sense of wonder, a desire to learn. I had a boss once whose philosophy was "If I haven't learned anything new in six months, there is something seriously wrong." He was an intelligent man and a flexible one. The expansive thinker is always flexible. So is the executive director of a meeting. He or she has to be because no two meetings are alike and people change every day. The audience you had last year won't be the same audience this year, even if it is made up of the same people.

What results does your organization want from its meeting? What are the best ways to get those results? Once you can answer those two fundamental questions, you will know how to organize successful meetings. The chapters that follow explore the different ways to find the answers.

1

DEFINING THE GOAL

I once organized a meeting for a restaurant company. The objective was to convince a group of franchisees that the company was fantastic. But the franchisees didn't believe this because their experience was that the company was poorly organized. My recommendation was that we meet the franchisees' concerns head-on, admit the shortcomings, and explain how the franchisees could help the company to improve. I suggested interviewing a representative cross section of the attendees before the meeting in order to have a clear understanding of their complaints. Then we could formulate answers and design the meeting as an open question-and-answer session.

The company rejected this plan and instead adopted a "good news" strategy. The meeting, however, turned out to be bad news. After the third senior executive had given an unbelievable speech about how rosy everything looked, the audience lost interest. Attendees began talking among themselves in side conversations. After the afternoon coffee break, nobody returned to the meeting. That evening's cocktail reception turned into a gripe session.

The next morning the atmosphere was tense and everybody was irritable. By the end of the day, the meeting had degenerated into a shouting match, with company executives and franchisees hurling accusations back and forth.

When I called the attendees as part of the follow-up process, I got an earful. Their main complaint was that the meeting didn't touch on any of their real concerns. The franchisees knew they weren't hearing the truth and the bad blood between them and the company continues to this day.

That meeting was doomed from the start because the

company had failed to define its goal clearly and realistically. Arriving at a properly defined goal is the first step in planning a successful meeting. Only when that is done can you determine the methods you will use to achieve that goal.

Focusing on the Problems

I like to think of a meeting's goal as a problem and the methods used to organize the meeting as the solution to that problem. Your problem might be how to motivate a sales force or fund-raising committee to work harder. Or how to improve communications. Or perhaps you need to make employees or members understand the long-term benefits of restructuring the organization. As "executive director" of your organization's meeting, it's your task to create solutions. But you can't create the right solutions unless you define the right problem.

As the leader of the senior executive team, you probably have formulated a strategic business plan for your organization. This is the place to start when deciding on your primary objective, the problem your meeting is going to solve. Review your long-term goals and consider how this meeting can help to achieve them. Perhaps there is a specific objective in the plan that is shouting out to be shared with everyone in the organization.

Take for example the president that I mentioned in the Introduction who wanted to introduce significant changes to his organization. His strategic business plan called for two separate elements: upgrading of systems and facilities, and having people think in new ways about the business. At the meeting itself he could only scratch the surface in imparting details of the actual physical and structural changes he was going to make. He therefore identified "a new way of thinking" as the primary objective of his conference. From this long-term strategic goal, he quickly and easily developed an appropriate three-part strategy of *convincing* people that it was time to change, *demonstrating* that everything was in place to facilitate those changes, and *guaranteeing* total support from the parent organization. This was an example of a clear and concise answer to a seemingly complex problem.

Another example is the story behind the memo presented here (Figure 1-1). The president of MegaCorp Inc. already had a successful and growing company. However, he was wisely aware of the tenuous nature of success. Therefore, his key strategic goal

Figure 1–1 The Executive Memo

To: Meeting Planning Executive
From: E. Jones, President, MegaCorp Inc.
Re: Our Upcoming Fall Conference

This memo will provide overall strategic focus to the executive. This should allow you to

1. identify the most effective and cost-efficient planning approach for the conference, and
2. communicate the intent of the plan to the coordination group.

MegaCorp Inc. has been enjoying rapid growth after the recession of a few years ago. Competition has increased and each new competitor has entered this crowded market with newer and improved products. MegaCorp Inc. has been slow to respond, but that will change.

We are about to embark on a Redevelopment Program that will take our strengths, product quality and high employee loyalty, and add to them dramatically improved sales and service systems, using

1. a new MIS program that will increase our strategic information tenfold
2. a new multi-level sales training program that will evolve over the next three years
3. a completely redesigned sales and marketing program to upgrade our image
4. a heavy capital reinvestment program that will increase our operations and delivery efficiency fourfold
5. a long-range employee communications program.

As you can see, we are keeping quality and loyalty while adding communications, style, efficiency, and marketing power.

It is time that we at the senior management level encourage all of our colleagues to share their ideas, perceptions, and knowledge with us and with each other. This networking will enrich our management skills and make our people feel that they *own* a part of this corporation. I am therefore instructing the planning executive to make arrangements for a conference that will allow most of our people to attend, at least for a portion of the event. Furthermore I want to set the following event objectives in priority:

1. Communicate the scope and nature of the changes that this organization will be undergoing.
2. Generate a positive attitude that will be shared by everyone.
3. Develop the five key areas identified in this memo for follow-up during the next twelve months.

I would like to suggest a starting theme: "Getting it *all* — together!"

I believe that we can make this change happen by working as a team. I look forward to receiving a meeting plan no later than three weeks from date of this memo. Thank you.

was to *strengthen* his company through information, education, capital investment, and internal communications. Of these four areas he correctly chose communications as the key goal for his meeting, because he recognized that his employees' high level of loyalty was a strength on which he could build. He wanted his people to feel that they "owned" a share of the corporation and therefore were directly involved in what was happening. In addition, he realized that action must always follow communications, because those communications comprise a *promise*.

Both of these presidents took a little time to think about the primary objective of their meetings — and the results were BIG.

How do you go about ensuring that you discover *your* primary objective? One way is to set goals unilaterally. As the person at the top, you can decide that you are going to educate the people in your organization about certain important facts of business life and call a meeting to do so. You can do this without ever asking them or anyone else what *they* think the meeting should be about. But the authoritarian approach to planning a meeting rarely brings good results.

Alternatively, you could gather information before you establish a primary objective. Using this approach, you could start out with a certain preliminary set of goals and, after doing some research and talking with your people, discover that those goals need some refinement.

For example, let's say that your primary goal is to identify the most promising members of your mid-management group for succession planning. You have been following the progress of certain individuals and it has become clear who is the best and who is the worst. However, these two extremes do not take into account those who might or might not have the "right stuff." So you've decided that a concentrated event like a meeting might be a good way to "shake the tree." Your goal is to identify whether there are suitable candidates in your organization to fill the total number of projected senior position vacancies for the next five years.

You can do research to discover whether this goal is realistic or achievable by

- talking to executives in other organizations who have faced and resolved such problems
- talking to your best people to see if they think that there are ways to tag other potentially successful candidates

- talking to human resource development consultants to see if there are concentrated ways of identifying successful executive potential
- selecting several candidates from your target group and interviewing them for their reactions

By taking these four steps, you will find out whether your goal is achievable. If it isn't, you will have to adopt a different, more appropriate goal.

Most organizations don't carry out this type of research. If they did, in my twenty years of planning meetings I would have organized dozens of events for the purpose of introducing computer technology to the workplace. The introduction of computers, after all, has been one of the biggest changes most organizations have experienced. Automation has a major impact on work arrangements, social relations within organizations, and career paths. Despite all the disruption it brings, many organizations just drop the new hardware into the plant or office. It can take months or years to iron out the problems that result.

There are thousands of organizations in North America that over the past few years should have held meetings directed at the smooth and effective introduction of computers. Yet only twice have I been asked to design such a meeting.

Adding the Executive Vision

Ideally, a meeting's goal is developed from a combination of audience research and your own personal vision. The knowledge and vision of an organization's executive are invaluable resources in the process of designing a meeting. But the views and the needs of the people who will be attending are also invaluable.

Would you launch a new product on the market without doing market research first? The product might be brilliantly conceived and built to the highest quality standards, but if nobody needs it, it's not going to sell. If your meeting doesn't fill the needs of your market — the people who are going to attend — it's guaranteed to flop.

A truly effective company president has a deep understanding of the industry in which the company operates. He or she has a penetrating vision of what the company should achieve. At the same time, the attendees of a meeting — whether employees, shareholders or colleagues — have certain needs that must be fulfilled if that vision is going to be realized. When your vision and your attendees' needs are joined, you have a powerful combination.

How do you incorporate vision and attendee needs? Start by looking at your organization. Look at your people, your vice presidents, yourself. What are the relationships in your company? Are they formal or informal? Are they based on human values or strictly materialistic ones? Is your corporate culture high-pressure or laid back? Is the management style person-to-person or highly bureaucratic? What is the history of the organization? What has made it succeed? When has it failed? What is planned for the future and why? What results are expected?

No two companies are alike. It's essential that your meetings reflect the most positive aspects of your organization, its people, its history, its philosophy.

Don't ignore the industry or field that you're in. Where does your organization fit within that area? What are its competitors like? How about your organization's products or services? Are they old or new? Where do your organization's marketing, advertising, and public relations position it? What do your public presentations say about the organization?

To be able to use the answers to all of these questions to define your goals, you must first understand that your meeting is going to take place on two levels: emotional and intellectual. The emotional level has to do with the "feel" of your organization — its "corporate culture." This is something intangible — an atmosphere, an environment, the subtleties of how your organization operates. Usually, the feel of an organization changes very little over time. But if there is a drastic change, such as a hostile takeover, it can change quickly.

If your meeting matches the feel of your organization, the attendees will be more comfortable and more ready to become involved than if it doesn't. They are in a strange place, away from home. Before they commit themselves to taking part fully in the meeting, they need some reassurance that this place and this meeting are part of an atmosphere in which they feel comfortable. If you can turn the meeting site into friendly territory, you've made an important first step toward gaining the attendees' commitment.

On the intellectual level, the attendees need concrete proof that the meeting will offer them something real that they can use. It's only by understanding your organization and your audience that you can be sure of fulfilling that need. Your meeting has to be a mirror image of your organization and it has to fulfill the needs of the audience. If it does those two things, it will be a success.

Identifying Your Audience

Once you've done your basic research, you can continue on to the discovery of your audience. That's not always as easy as it might seem. Sometimes it requires an intuitive reading of what people are telling you. People aren't always as frank as you would like and for that reason you have to read between the lines.

What are your audience's likes and dislikes? Where and when do they do their best work? What turns them on and off? What is their orientation? Are most of them happiest dealing with other people or are they more comfortable absorbing facts and figures in written form? The best way to find out is by distributing questionnaires, a subject we'll be discussing in a later chapter.

What issues are most important to them? What do they think they need: training? more attention from management? better equipment? more money? What are their commitments? Are they committed to the organization's philosophy? If not, what would it take to gain their commitment?

A good way to gather this type of sensitive information is to take some of your people on a retreat — perhaps to somebody's country cottage or to an informal resort hotel. Leave suits, ties, and corporate mythology behind and replace them with jeans, sport shirts, and plain talk.

Often people are much more willing to open up when they're away from the office. If there are problems in operations, administration, fund-raising, or sales and they all stem from the same source — a management that is out of touch with its staff — that will come out. Problems become easy to identify when people are honest.

If a retreat isn't possible, try getting together a team representing the different divisions within your organization. Have the team members ask their colleagues the kinds of questions listed above. Then have management and the team sit down together for a report on what has been learned. Spend an afternoon discussing it openly and frankly. Absorb the information and think about it for a few days.

At the end of that process, you should be in a position to begin formulating objectives for the meeting and strategies for realizing those objectives. In order to achieve positive results, the objectives should be as precise as possible.

Building the Right Meeting

Building a meeting is like building a house. A house provides shelter and, in a way, so does a meeting. Just as a house protects its inhabitants against outside elements such as rain and wind, a meeting is a sheltered experience; it protects its participants from interference and distraction while they work together to achieve a goal.

A house is built of pieces of lumber or of bricks and mortar. A meeting is built of training sessions, business games, guest speakers, question-and-answer sessions, workshops, and panel discussions. Just as bricks and mortar will produce a good house only if they are skillfully assembled, a meeting must have the appropriate elements assembled in the right way. If it doesn't, it won't achieve its goal.

Communications are the architecture of a meeting. Designing a meeting, like designing a building, is to a large extent a process of selection and elimination. You select those elements that will help you to achieve your goal and eliminate all others. If you walk into a school or an office tower or a house, you don't have to be told what the primary purpose is for each building. What these structures are for is obvious from the design, from what's been put in and what's been left out.

It's true that a school can be used for community activities or to stage entertainment events. But its primary purpose, as a place for educating people, is obvious. Similarly, while a meeting might be called to achieve two or more purposes, it must have a primary objective that is immediately clear to everyone present.

Some meetings are intended to educate, others to motivate. Some are for decision making, others are for problem solving. The architecture of your meeting depends entirely on its primary purpose. That's why "Know Thy Purpose" is the first commandment of meeting design.

A house can be used as a hospital in an emergency. It could also be used as a school. But it's not as good for those purposes as a building that's designed to be a hospital or a school. The house's primary purpose is as a residence for a family, and that's the purpose it serves best. One of the biggest mistakes people make in planning meetings is to load them with too many objectives. If you try to use one meeting for education *and* motivation *and* decision making *and* rest and relaxation, the danger is that you'll do none of these well.

There's a simple test to tell you if your goal is precise enough. Could you measure after the meeting to find out if your goal was achieved? Suppose your goal is to improve peoples' attitudes. Can you measure that accurately? Probably not.

If, however, your goal is that by the end of the meeting, eighty percent of your people will have a positive attitude on one specific issue, then you're in business. That's a good, precise objective. It can be measured easily by talking to a hundred percent of the people. If eight out of ten have the positive attitude you wanted, your meeting is a success. If they don't, at least you know they don't. And that's better than living in a dream world.

Creating Solutions

Once you've defined the problem properly, your next step is to develop a process for creating the right solutions. The word "process" suggests development. It means starting from a certain point and expanding outward, increasing the complexity, adding new steps and new elements, and integrating it all into a coherent whole.

You are the starting point and once you've answered the question "What should be done?" you're ready to answer a second question: "How should it be accomplished?"

Let's take a closer look at this in terms of a real situation. I did a meeting for a fast-food company whose goal was to stimulate the thinking of its people. That might sound vague, but it wasn't. In the past, this company's meetings had been for relaxation purposes only — a lot of drinking, a lot of chitchatting, and not much else. Now the company was expanding during a time when it was experiencing intense competition, and management wanted to get people thinking about the company and their role in it. My first step was to find out what management meant when it talked about "stimulating people's thinking." It turned out to mean developing an emotional attachment to the company.

How did the company want its people to be emotionally attached? Well, it seemed the employees were taking the company for granted. Some of them had been there for twenty-five years and they saw no connection other than history between themselves and the company. Working with management, I finally defined our goal, or problem, as redefining the company in the minds of the staff. We wanted the employees to experience the company not just as a good old standby, a crutch, a guaranteed security blanket. We wanted them to see working for the company as a challenge — a challenge to themselves to strive continuously for improvement. We were looking for three kinds of improvement: in their attitudes toward themselves, their jobs, and the company; in their handling of their jobs; and in the way they dealt with customers, staff, and management. If they could improve themselves in these ways, the company would be improved in the process.

This was a big job and we decided that the best approach was to give them a good message about themselves. The message was "You can realize a lot more potential than you ever thought you had." We defined the theme of the meeting as "Rise above the Rest": rise above other people, rise above themselves, and develop within themselves positive attributes that they never knew they had.

The next step was to find the best way to communicate that message. What could we do to create a personal experience that would bring the message to life in a way that a lecture could not? We decided to send the people "above the rest" literally — in a hot-air balloon. This was a brand-new experience for them and one that involved risk taking. The balloon theme was part of a whole range of activities involving competition that took place every day. Others included baseball games, water sports, tennis, volleyball, golf tournaments, and a business game.

Our guest speaker was an astronaut, Colonel Jack Lousma, who talked about the satisfactions of taking risks and overcoming fear. By the end of the meeting, we wanted people to be saying, "Yes, it's true, I am capable of being better than I have been."

The day-to-day business of this company, like that of most companies, wasn't exciting or adventurous. Usually it was bland and predictable. But we wanted people to see that challenges exist even though you might not be aware of them. The purpose of the ballooning adventure and the astronaut's speech was to demonstrate that life doesn't have to be boring. If you want to take charge and develop as a person, identify obstacles and overcome them, then you have to approach each day with a feeling of excitement. After twenty-five years of working at the same place, that's awfully hard to do and it doesn't happen overnight.

But in interviewing ten percent of the attendees at the closing reception and in other interviews after the meeting we satisfied ourselves that we had succeeded in sending our audience away from the conference with certain germinal ideas. This meeting was the first in a series that will take place over several years to heighten employee sensitivity to many issues. As the first step in a long-term development strategy, it was a great success.

Hot-air balloons to change people's thinking? For some, that's just so much hot air. In my opinion, it's a good example of strategic thinking. Strategic thinking is long-range thinking, and as executive director your ambition should be to produce an event that will have long-range, positive effects.

Inherent in strategic thinking is intuitiveness and creativity. For this you require a thorough knowledge of your organization and your audience. Intuitiveness isn't just luck; it's based on knowledge. That knowledge may have been absorbed years ago, but it comes out when it's needed. The more knowledgeable you are, the more creative you can be.

In creating strategy, we use two systems of logic: deductive and inductive. Deductive logic takes us from the general to the specific, from research about your organization and your audience to specific goals for the meeting. Inductive logic works in the opposite direction. You start from the goals and develop strategies for achieving them.

It's important that the deductive logic be applied first, that your research be conducted with an open mind. One of the big mistakes planners make is applying inductive logic too soon in the planning process. They come to the research process with preconceived ideas and they look for confirmation. Although they don't get it, they still cling to their original ideas. They believe so strongly in these preconceived ideas that they charge full speed ahead — and the attendees are left shaking their heads in bewilderment at a program that doesn't address any of their needs.

The inductive stage is much harder than the deductive because it calls for creativity and imagination. I did a project for a moving firm that wanted to improve its salespeople's ability to sell the company's services to corporate head offices. These salespeople were good at what they called "sofa sales" — sitting down with a family at home and arranging to move that family anywhere in the world. But if they had to go into a corporate head office they would seize up.

Our goal was well defined: increase sales in the corporate market by several million dollars per year. Knowing the goal, we then proceeded to develop a strategy. Clearly, what these salespeople needed to be effective in the head office environment was education, training, and motivation.

We developed a theme: "2 + 2 = 5." There's obviously something wrong with this equation, and that's exactly what we wanted the salespeople to point out. We began the meeting by explaining the theme through a multi-image slide show describing the four major ingredients of a successful marketing effort: product, price, promotion, and place. Then we said that there was a missing item, number five, which is the people who make up the sales force. In order to make the other four ingredients work, those people must have their acts together.

After the slide show, the president of the company spoke. He outlined the three main points on the agenda: education, training, and motivation. Potential corporate head office clients addressed the meeting to tell the salespeople what they needed in a transportation service. A new computer-based, cost-estimation system was introduced, along with some new printed promotional materials for the corporate market.

Then came the training phase, which included a seminar oriented toward selling to corporate executives and dealing with such issues as financial presentations, preparing written proposals, and closing skills.

The final section of the meeting, on motivation, featured Martin Rutte, president of a California-based personal management organization, who spoke about linking what the attendees had just learned to their own personal goals. Using simple exercises and examples, he was able to place the entire content of the meeting into a package that was relevant to the personal needs of each attendee.

Seven Steps to a Winning Strategy

Let's itemize the seven steps in developing a strategy.

Research, Research, Research — Step number one is research. Dig deeply. Don't assume anything. Talk to your colleagues, friends, and business acquaintances. Honestly accept and weigh whatever you discover even if it seems to conflict with what you've believed to be the truth until then. This can be a wonder-fully enlightening and liberating exercise if you keep ego and personal insecurity out of it.

When I first began in the communications business, I encountered a corporate vice president who was absolutely sure of everything. My job was to help him plan a training seminar for a forest industry association to help operators reduce downtime on some new equipment. His approach was to rap the operators on the knuckles, telling them that the way they had been proceeding was all wrong, and insisting that they follow a certain list of rules. I thought that, rather than imposing one viewpoint in a dictatorial fashion, it would be more effective simply to explain the advantages of alternate procedures in a thoughtful, businesslike manner. But the client had his way and the session was so unsuccessful that it had to be repeated.

The lesson is that you have to be sensitive to your audience. In planning a meeting, talk to people, send out questionnaires, listen, and analyze what you find out. You might be surprised at what you discover. The annual convention for a voluntary association had always been a low-key, casual affair; everyone assumed that's what the members wanted. But when I sent out a simple questionnaire before one annual convention, the responses indicated overwhelmingly that the majority wanted a more professional event, the better to justify the expense of attending. So we upgraded the convention with a big theme, more activities, and more elaborate opening and closing ceremonies.

Concentrate on the Problem — Step number two is defining the problem. You've evolved your objectives and now you rephrase everything in terms of the problem. Once I consulted on the preparations for a chemical company's meeting. The planners were in a quandary. The president's orders were to "do something and make it cheap." They didn't know what that "something" was; they had no goal.

We interviewed fifteen executives and attendees and identified an excellent goal that we defined as a problem: How do we get everyone to join in solving six fundamental market and sales problems the company is now facing? Once we had a goal and a problem to solve, everything fell into place.

Look at All Solutions — Step number three is examining every possible way of solving the problem, from the conservative to the crazy. The purpose of this exercise is to free up your thinking so that you don't get boxed into preconceived notions. Don't try to do this by yourself. You need other people — preferably people who don't think the way you do.

In the case of the chemical company, we came up with three possible ways of attacking the problem. One was to take a brainstorming approach in which we would ask everyone to generate as many ideas as possible, including weird and wacky ones. The second was to bring in an expert facilitator who could motivate everyone into solving the problem. The third was to send out clear, written definitions to all the attendees beforehand and ask them to bring prepared analyses to the meeting.

Make Your Strategy Fit — Step number four is coming up with what I call the "right fit," a strategy that feels right, that lets you say to yourself, "Yes, I know this is going to work because it's hitting all the problem areas."

For the chemical company, the right fit was a combination of the first and third proposed strategies. We used brainstorming techniques to further enhance the individually prepared solutions and recommendations.

This approach fit because it was in line with the company's desire to make its employees think for themselves and because it satisfied the president's order to keep costs down. It also felt more comfortable because management was anxious to keep outsiders out of discussions of some touchy and confidential issues.

Do a Reality Test — Step number five involves reality testing. What is the worst thing that could possibly happen? What is the best? Reality usually falls somewhere between the two. Make sure that the fit still feels good after you've done this exercise.

A medical supplies company that had just been bought out by its own senior management had to select a strategy for a meeting on how to motivate its salespeople to take on the competition more aggressively. The strategy it chose was based on the concept of growth. The meeting would try to demonstrate how the other major competitor was growing and how our people had to do more to achieve similar growth in our company.

When we reality-tested this concept, we decided that the worst thing that could happen would be that our people would become demoralized and say, "This competitor is growing so fast that we can't compete against him." The best thing would be that they would say, "OK, if those guys can do it, so can we."

The reality would likely be a mixture of both responses. Before going ahead with the strategy, we had to decide whether that probable result would produce the motivated sales force we wanted. We ultimately decided that it would if we designed the communications in the meeting to address both types of responses. The meeting unfolded as we had predicted and was successful.

Carry Through with Detail — Step number six is where the hard work comes in because it involves extending your strategy to every single detail of the meeting. As the original goals become strategies to solve problems, your planning begins to incorporate the complex mechanisms that are needed to make the meeting actually happen. These mechanisms include master execution plans and the myriad logistical details that directly touch each individual's personal experience of the event. Each one of these mechanisms must be "on strategy."

In the case of the moving company, our strategy was education, training, and motivation. Therefore, when we set up the registration table, it was laid out in just that way — educational materials, training materials, and motivational materials. Every single element has to fit the strategy. Is the prospective guest speaker an educational, training, or motivational person? If not, he doesn't belong on the agenda of this meeting.

Plan to Measure Results — Step number seven is to build bridges between the strategy and the objectives, to make certain that what you do obtains the desired results. That means coming up with a way to measure those results. For example, if your goal is to solve the problem of how to overcome the inroads made by a competitor, your meeting will be successful to the degree that you come up with ideas about how to counterattack.

Perhaps the competitor is hurting you in three ways: lower price, better service, and quicker delivery. Your goal might be to come up with ten workable ideas to counterattack in each area. Formulating your goals in such a quantifiable fashion makes measuring results a straightforward matter. The follow-up, long-range measurement is how well these ideas work compared with how well you expected them to work. The real value of those thirty ideas you came up with won't be known for some time. It usually takes one fiscal year to get an adequate reading on the results of a meeting.

Once you've figured out how you're going to measure your results, you are ready to organize your meeting.

2

ORGANIZING FOR ACTION

You have set out a strategic direction that you want to follow. Now how are you going to ensure that the people you delegate to handle the nuts and bolts of the meeting actually go in the direction you want? How can you guarantee that the result is the successful meeting you've envisioned?

The basic elements of a meeting are logistics, communications, and strategic design. Logistics are the items that everyone normally thinks of first in relation to meeting planning: hotels, travel, meals, printed materials, equipment, etc. These are the "hardware" of the event and must be coordinated carefully to work well.

Two types of communications are involved in any meeting, and both are very important. The first type of communications, content, includes not only the content of the meeting program but also the invitations, welcoming letters, flyers, and whatever other types of media you have chosen to communicate with the attendees both before and during the meeting. The second type is environmental communications — the *feeling* that is transmitted to the attendees by the environment of the meeting, both physical and the feeling conveyed by the program itself. For example, the program of a rest-and-relaxation meeting would transmit a very different feeling than an all-business meeting, and a different setting would be chosen in which to hold each type of meeting.

The "feeling" of a meeting is dictated by your goals and the strategic design that you evolve to meet these goals. As the executive director of the meeting you chose the germinal strategic design that affects all of the other elements of the meeting. This basic strategic design will expand and grow into the complex event that your meeting will be. But for the meeting to turn out the way you want, the design must contain all of the information necessary to produce the finished product.

Before you pass your strategic design down to the people who will actually plan and coordinate your meeting, you must shape it so that it acts as a filter that automatically eliminates inappropriate options. I recommend that you do this through a memo containing a comprehensive description of exactly what the meeting should achieve and why. An example of such a memo is presented in Figure 1–1 (page 3). This memo will activate the next phase of the meeting's development. It must be so clear that the planners and coordinators reading it can readily distinguish between correct and incorrect planning choices.

Casting the Production

Just as important as getting the memo right is finding the right people to carry out the instructions the memo will contain. To successfully plan your meeting you will need a team of specialists who share your understanding of the organization, who are flexible and willing to compromise, and who are able to think for themselves and make decisions. These are the people who will shoulder much of the day-to-day responsibility of producing a meeting that is "on strategy." They must be people in whose abilities you have confidence or whose credentials prove that they are up to the job.

Planning and conducting a large meeting is a complex communications job and not one that can be left to inexperienced clerical or secretarial staff. This is too often the case and the result is meetings that inevitably lack spark. The people planning and organizing them may well have talent but they don't have the authority to design a meeting that delivers a powerful message.

Your group must be a team, not a committee. A team has an acknowledged leader who establishes a direction and pursues it with discipline and precision. I know from experience how dangerous it can be to leave important decisions to a committee. A division of a large chemical company asked me to present some ideas for a senior management conference. The president of the division had set up a committee to plan the event but hadn't given the committee any clear directions. The committee at first approved enthusiastically when I suggested using an outstanding keynote speaker and an agenda related to the speaker's ideas. But before long, a debate arose over whether the president would like the speaker. Both men were high-profile, powerful individuals with strong ideas and well-defined styles. But they hadn't met. Would they be compatible?

After considerable waffling, the committee decided to accept the agenda but not the speaker. Since the whole direction of the conference revolved around the personality and message of that individual, I strongly objected to this compromise but was over-ruled.

After the event was over, the president called to complain about how poorly it had gone. His original intent to motivate and energize his senior managers hadn't been carried out. Mv defense was that his committee had rejected my recommendation to bring in an outstanding speaker. The committee had been empowered to stand in for him without having a clear strategy to guide it.

For the next year's conference I urged him to establish a team with himself as the leader. He did so and the result was a much more productive conference at a lower cost. You should follow the same course in planning your meeting. Don't set up a committee with more leaders than followers. You need an effective team made up of members oriented toward accomplishing a task that you've clearly defined.

Assigning the Roles

The people on your meeting team should have demonstrated intelligence and creativity in performing other tasks. They should also have a minimal need for ego gratification. This means that they will understand quickly how to get things done within the context of your strategy. You don't want people who only tolerate working with others; you want people who *love* working with others. This is an imperative. In producing a meeting, someone who likes people can produce ten times as much as the most talented lone wolf.

Your team members also should share similar attitudes toward important business issues. Office politics make for incompatible bedfellows and a struggle for power will be harmful. For this reason, avoid political appointments. Just because someone is a senior member of your organization it doesn't mean that he or she belongs on your team. If he or she lacks the time, expertise, or required people-skills, you won't get the smooth teamwork you need.

When you've got the right people, the first step is to make certain that each understands his or her responsibilities, the limits of that responsibility, and the necessity of working to schedule.

Your team should be divided into three distinct subgroups to handle the three distinct phases of conducting a large meeting: planning, production, and follow-up. The planning team members need different talents from those who will make the actual hands-on arrangements. And the production team should not be assigned to assess and follow up the results because their bias toward operations will hamper their ability to be objective. Some members of the planning team should also play a role in the follow-up, a topic that will be discussed in detail in a later chapter.

As you will see below, a meeting in its early planning stage should be treated as a marketing program. Therefore, you will need people who understand marketing principles and have the imagination to apply them to a meeting. You will also need people to take charge of the five logistical elements: travel, registration, food and accommodation, entertainment, and special programs. All of these will be described in later chapters.

Should you restrict your team to members of your own organization? Not necessarily. Organizations that keep their meeting planning exclusively in-house can lose touch with trends and deprive themselves of the objectivity that good consultants can provide. Maintaining specialists on the payroll can be more expensive than hiring a consultant on an occasional basis. As a rule, I suggest adding one qualified outsider to your group to provide the broadening benefits of a different background and experience.

As I've already made clear, I believe a meeting should be run by a team led by an executive director who is the senior executive of the organization. However, there are other options. A common one is the one-man show, in which a qualified professional meeting planner on your staff is assigned to do whatever is necessary to produce the meeting. His or her plans often run into resistance from other organization members who get involved, but if this meeting planner has an extremely hard head, it can work.

Another option is to use independent consultants. Some of these are strong on the design side while others specialize in logistics. A pair of consultants, one to design and the other to put the nuts and bolts in place, is often the best solution. But if you leave yourself entirely out of the planning process, you are paying for something that may not be to your liking. Don't undervalue your own vision and insights into your organization. These are more valuable than any meeting planner's experience.

Marketing Your Meeting

Your team's first step will be to launch a marketing campaign. A meeting is like a new product: it's an unknown. Its consumers are the people who will attend the meeting. What they are looking for is a special event that gets special results. You'll always get a result out of a meeting. But will you get the result you want?

Let's consider the similarities to marketing more closely. Marketing is a mix of the "four Ps" — product, price, promotion, and place. Product, in the context of a meeting, is the message you are trying to get across. The "customers" for this "product," of course, are the people who attend the meeting. One or two members of your team should become product experts. They should be assigned to investigate every angle of the message that you want to communicate. They should report back to you on how a representative sample of the audience has reacted to it, what fine tuning is required, and how best the message can be presented.

What does a meeting product look like? In a rest-and-relaxation meeting, or one held to show appreciation for an all-out campaign effort,the product is a message that the attendees take home with them: "We had a great time thanks to the organization." In a meeting dedicated to solving production problems, the product is this message: "Thanks to the company, from now on production will be easier for everyone."

As a marketer, you have to hammer home the relationship between the meeting and your organization. Over the course of many meetings, that positive identification adds up to long-term loyalty.

Price is the time, effort, and money that it costs people to attend your meeting. The benefits they gain from the meeting have to be worth the price. Another member of your team should have the job of assessing this relationship.

Promotions include such advertising items as pre-meeting memos and packages, banners and other decor items at the meeting itself, imprinted pads and pencils, audio-visual shows, and skits. Promotions are the sizzle on the steak. Meetings need color and sound. They should energize the people in attendance.

Place, in marketing terms, refers to the distribution of goods into different regions. In a meeting, it means the location in which your message is delivered. This is not a trivial matter. People are affected by their environment. Where you deliver your message is part of the message. A member of your team will be responsible for choosing a location suitable to your meeting strategy.

One company's message was "Let's all have fun and get to know one another." It then proceeded to keep its people in the basement meeting room of a resort hotel for ten solid hours. The resort location actually was in line with the company's message. But the meeting itself gave another message: "Let's work even harder than we usually do back at the office." By the end of the day, the attendees had no energy left to enjoy the great outdoors. They were too tired to do anything but sleep.

Market your meeting as you might market a product. Make it appealing and interesting. Promise something you know you can deliver and then, through careful design, deliver it.

Selecting Your Communications Tools

Communications are the essence of a meeting. If there is a breakdown in communications, you don't have a meeting at all. You will need a capable person with experience in communications or advertising to take charge.

This person will have some difficult decisions to make. He or she has to choose the right communications vehicles from among audio-visual materials, guest speakers, workshops, open forums, panel discussions, industrial theater, and business games. From among interactive computer programs, workbooks, and special printed materials. From among banners, posters, props, room decorations, pins, registration badges, and tags.

I like to imagine the different communications media at a meeting as a series of concentric circles (see Figure 2–1). The media represented by the innermost circles are the ones that interact most powerfully with the attendees.

The outermost circle is the pre-meeting teaser campaign designed to generate curiosity about the event and to lead to emotional and intellectual involvement. Letters and lapel pins are among the items that can be used as teasers.

Once I organized a meeting that had as its theme "New Horizons." The goal was to identify new sales opportunities and ways to exploit them. As teasers, we used imitation passports with the attendees' names in them. The passports were accompanied by letters that suggested people get ready to venture into new territories. As the meeting progressed, we stamped the passports at various functions, and when all of them were fully stamped they went into a drum for a draw to win a Caribbean cruise.

The next circle includes such decor items as banners, props, and name tags. All of these things should have a cohesive look. A graphics specialist can present several options based on your theme.

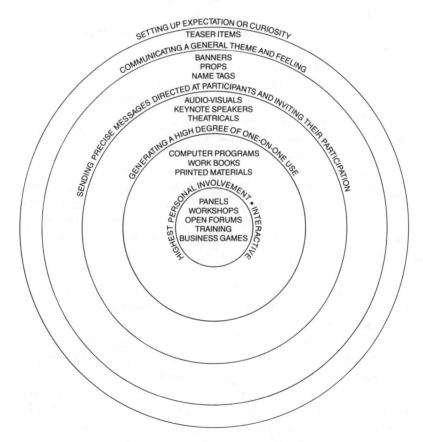

Figure 2-1 Communications Tools

Yet another circle includes audio-visuals, keynote speakers, and other forms of staged communications that impart a precise message. You need a clear idea of what you want to say and how you want to say it; these will be precisely defined in your strategic direction memo. Just as you would look at a storyboard and rushes before allowing your advertising agency to air a commercial, you should insist on seeing scripts for all meeting presentations, audio-visuals, and theatricals to ensure that they are on strategy.

The next circle includes computer programs, workbooks, and special printed materials for learning or information. These items must be usable by a broad range of different people and should be put together by specialists.

The final, most interactive, circle includes workshops, open forums, training sessions, business games, and panel discussions. These communications vehicles get people involved in a personal way. The only sure way to design them properly is to try out some prototypes on a representative sample of attendees and refine them through trial and error.

How do you decide which communications tools to use? Your strategic design decides for you. That is why you formulated your strategy first. Take the case of the company we described in the last chapter that wanted to develop a risk-taking spirit among longtime employees who had become cautious and settled in their ways.

These people weren't sensitive to the changes taking place in the company as it expanded in a much more competitive market. The company was developing new corporate strategies to address customer needs, to design new products, and to deal with customers. But employee attitudes were lagging behind boardroom strategy.

The larger theme, "Rise above the Rest," which I described in the last chapter, was chosen because the employees were a subdued and conservative lot. They weren't risk takers and that was a problem for a company in the throes of expansion. The strategy and the nature of the audience determined the communications vehicle we finally chose, a specially created audio-visual about hot-air ballooning. Our guest speaker, astronaut Jack Lousma, was able to relate the risks and problems that astronauts face to the individual employee in the store. The audience found his speech fascinating and peppered him with questions about risk and fear.

In addition, we put together a series of business games, each of which involved risk and chance, constantly reinforcing the notion that risk is part of life, even when you're working behind the counter of a store. The whole concept was further emphasized in written materials. And the people responded. They said we had told them something they hadn't been thinking about and yes, there is a risk in trying to reach out, to become more interested in customers as individuals, to develop new leads, to get out and investigate the competition, to become more involved in the community.

This meeting was one in which the strategic design was simple but in which the methods of communication had to be carefully selected. It was a specific combination of communications elements that produced the desired results.

But the best communications package would not have done the job had the logistics been carelessly handled. To this point, I've been downplaying logistics because I believe they are the last thing with which you, the senior executive, should concern yourself. But that doesn't mean they're not important. It means that once your strategic design is in place and once you've chosen your communications package, you're finally ready to make intelligent decisions about where you should hold the meeting, how many people should be invited, how you're going to get them there, what type of rooms you'll need, and how you're going to schedule it all.

The Psychology of Logistics

Why do we save the logistics for last? Because doing so is a surefire way of avoiding the trap into which so many meeting planners fall and that is *failing to stick ruthlessly to strategy*.

You've worked hard to come up with a strategic approach and if you don't stick to it you've wasted your time. If in the "Rise above the Rest" example we had staged the meeting in a small, cramped room to save money, we would have been at odds with our strategy of presenting a company in an exciting and risky phase of expansion. Room size was determined by strategy.

It was important that when the employees went up in the hot-air balloon they experience the thrill associated with risk taking. That determined the answer to the logistical question of when to send the balloon up. We decided against using the balloon on the first day of the meeting because there was no breeze and the flight would have been too calm. On the second day, there was a wind and a good opportunity for a thrilling flight. Logistics took second place to strategy, instead of the other way around.

If we had decided to bring in a clown after Jack Lousma had spoken, just because the clown was available and was a lot of fun, we would have blundered because the clown would have contributed nothing to our strategy.

Some people love entertainment for its own sake but unless the entertainment advances your objectives, it has no place in your logistics. In most meetings that I design there is an entertainment evening. Sometimes we will bring in entertainment that has no relation to the meeting's content, but that's deliberately done to provide a mental break.

What too often happens is that meeting planners sprinkle a little of that here and a little of this there with the result that too much randomly chosen entertainment detracts from the overall design of the meeting. Stick ruthlessly to strategy. You may love an idea but if it doesn't fit your strategy, don't put it into your meeting.

Measuring Results

The measuring of results is all the more important when you're taking a strategic approach because you need to know if your objectives have been achieved. I like to set up measurement criteria right at the beginning of the whole process. These criteria should be part of your strategic direction memo.

In Chapter 7, "Follow-up for Future Planning," I discuss methods that reinforce positive meeting results and/or identify areas that require more input during the following year. Measuring your meeting results yields the basic information required for the follow-up process.

People might say, "The meeting was terrific," but how do you know whether they've experienced any significant change as a result of the experience? Because people will say one thing and do another, the only sure way to measure change is behavioral. Your standards of measurement have to be based on performance.

Suppose you wanted to change attendee attitudes with regard to risk taking. There are lists of words that relate closely to a risk-taking mentality. If we ask someone before a meeting to write down the first thing that comes to mind when he hears the word "risk" and he responds, "Raiders of the Lost Ark," we know that person has had no real experience of risk taking and doesn't really understand what it is. But if, after the meeting, he writes something like "extending yourself," then you know that significant change has taken place. This is more than an intellectual exercise because if a person's thinking changes, his performance usually will change as well.

Our goal in the "Rise above the Rest" meeting, for example, was to heighten sensitivity as measured by the participants' responses at the end of the meeting, and to do that we had to measure their responses at the beginning. This was easy to do in a questionnaire by asking, "How many regular customers do you know by their first names? How frequently do regular customers come into your store? How much do you know about your competition and how they deal with your customers? How much do you know about your company and its place in the market?"

At the end of the meeting we needed to know if there had been a significant change in employee knowledge and sensitivity. We were able to measure it through such questions as "What do you plan to do about your customers and customer contact? How concerned are you about being in touch with what your company is doing?" Measuring the difference between the two sets of responses was a straightforward task.

In the case of an actual performance change, your standards of measurement are going to be different. Suppose your goal is to get your salespeople to increase their close rate. At present they are seeing twenty clients per week and are closing on three of them, for a rate of fifteen percent. You're after a twenty percent rate. Your objective could not be more clearly defined: you want your salesmen to show a five percent increase per week, from three closes to four. This can go into your memo as a clearly defined objective. The strategy might then be to build the meeting around a business game designed to improve closing skills and to develop at least five new closing techniques.

But how are you going to make sure that those five new closes have been well learned by the time your people leave the room? If you wait until they're out in the field performing, you might find that some of them haven't absorbed the new information. You can retrain them or fire them, but it's better to test them first. It's not difficult to prepare a short exam that will illustrate situations in which the five new closes can be used. If you find, for example, that one person doesn't understand the material, you can provide the remedial work sooner rather than later. This process of testing and monitoring should begin before the meeting ends. And in your memo, you should indicate the importance of having this happen.

It's most important to prepare standards of measurement before you start your meeting, and to have measurement tools that you can use immediately after. Measure as quickly as possible, because the longer you let it go, the more likely it is that it won't get done. And if it doesn't get done, you really don't know whether your meeting was useful or not. If you state all of this clearly your team will get the message and perform up to your expectations. If you've chosen them wisely and given them the right combination of direction and authority, they will help you to guarantee a successful meeting.

3

PRODUCING SIGNIFICANT CHANGE

Significant change is long-term behavioral change that produces long-term results. How do you produce change that will last for months or years during the course of a meeting that will last only a few days at most? The answer is, by giving the people attending the meeting a good reason to get involved in the long-range plans. And that means getting them thoroughly involved in the meeting itself.

Like a machine, a meeting can be analyzed in terms of its moving parts (the logistics) and the operational principles that govern the design of those moving parts. These operational principles include the four main purposes for calling meetings: transmission of information, problem solving, learning, and motivation. They also include the ways in which people interact when they are together. We'll analyze these under the broad categories of group dynamics, cooperation and competition, and hierarchies. Your team should be able to identify and use these basic operational principles of large meetings before it starts working out the logistical details.

Transmitting Information

Significant change won't be achieved unless new information and new ideas are absorbed by the attendees. Meetings are learning experiences and it's the design team's job to ensure that information is transmitted in the most effective way possible. To do that, you must give people a good reason for learning.

If a child is plunked into a French class in school and sees no reason for learning the language, studying French will be a low priority for the child. If, on the other hand, the child's family moved to France, he or she would need French to communicate with other children when playing or to order food in a restaurant. The child would quickly become French-speaking.

THE TEASE

The communications effort starts before the meeting begins. It starts with the "tease." A teaser or "tickle" campaign does several things, one of which is to cause excitement. It gets people hepped up. A good example was a teaser campaign a couple of years ago for the remake of a horror movie, *The Fly*. Mysterious little ads popped up all over the newspapers. One of them said, "Help me," and there was a little picture of a fly in the corner of the ad. People's interest was piqued.

The most powerful messages are also the shortest. A good example is Winston Churchill's "V for Victory." In one simple hand signal, Churchill encapsulated volumes of information about Britain, about the Germans, and about the war. Churchill was running a military campaign, not a teaser campaign. But "V for Victory" could be an excellent teaser for a political party going into a convention that it hopes will be a step on the road to power or for a company planning to take on a powerful adversary in the marketplace. This is the type of powerful metaphor that is needed.

A teaser campaign should generate questions but not confusion. Often a meeting planner will make the mistake of sending out a teaser that has a cute line but fails to inform the attendees of what's expected of them. I did a meeting for a food company with the purpose of introducing a new sales team to the company. We sent out a tiny invitation that said "Join the team. Make the best get better?" That told them we expected them to join the team. The question mark had them wondering about what was meant by "best." Did it mean the sales staff, the products, or the entire company?

The teaser succeeded in getting the participants thinking before the meeting got underway. How can the best get better? If this company is already the best, then how are we going to fit in? A teaser campaign is like preparing the soil before you seed it. We had the participants' attention *before* they checked in at the meeting.

A teaser campaign should lead to what I call a "mini-conclusion." It should contain questions but people should be able to answer those questions. At the meeting, their conclusions are going to be reinforced and they will have a vested interest in being involved. If you've ever done crossword puzzles, you'll understand what I mean by a vested interest. When you finish a puzzle successfully, you feel a sense of satisfaction. You want to do another, perhaps not immediately, but soon.

Your attendees will experience the same feelings when they successfully solve the riddles or puzzles that you present in your teaser campaign. When we feel good we seek more of those good feelings. We are energized by positive feedback and we're more open to positive reinforcement.

Many people have attended a lot of silly meetings where they were promised a lot of things that were not delivered. As a result, the planning team may have to overcome a certain amount of defensiveness and skepticism. By creating good feelings, your teaser campaign can help you to do that. People begin to network about the upcoming meeting because they have something positive in common to talk about. They have a vested interest in maintaining that sense of togetherness. Raising the level of vested interest is one of the most important mechanisms you have for controlling the meeting.

While meetings are in progress, the attendees look for a sense of togetherness and harmony; they are always concerned that harmony will decay into individualism and small group confusion. The more that you as the meeting planner are the cause of the participant's feelings of togetherness, the more control you have over them and what you want them to do.

When the attendees depend on you for the positive feelings that the meeting is generating, they are more responsive and open to the changes you want them to experience. It's a sort of ownership that is first offered to them through the teaser campaign, then crystallized by the first positive impressions they get at the meeting, and finally is solidified by the constant reinforcement, hour after hour, day after day, of the events on the agenda.

A teaser campaign should raise people's level of attention and consciousness. Perhaps your organization has a problem with competition. You have one perception of the competition and the staff has another. Your planning group's goal is to make them more conscious of the competitive challenge. The teaser campaign is an important first step in that process.

I worked as part of a group for a client in the pharmaceutical business that was locked in a competitive struggle with two other major players in a narrow product spectrum. The client wanted to stress the closeness of the competition and the ever-present need for its sales staff to operate at full throttle.

To bring the point home we planned a teaser campaign in which a small checkered flag, about 5 by 3 inches (12.5 x 7.5 cm), was mailed to each attendee. It said, "Start your engines."

A few weeks later we sent out a set of racing sunglasses with the message "The race is on!" printed on the carrying case. Included with the glasses was a checklist of items relating to the different competitive situations they faced as salespeople. We called this the "pit crew check." We asked each recipient to consider each point and write a little note describing how he or she had responded to the situation or would respond to it. The completed list went back to head office for use during the meeting.

The final part of the teaser campaign was sent off a week before the meeting. It was a key chain, again featuring the checkered flag motif and containing the statement "Push it to the floor!" The teaser campaign succeeded in preparing the attendees to think of what they were doing as salespeople in terms of the fierce competition of a car race in which every second counts. They arrived ready and willing to hear about the new approaches the company was taking to meet the competition head-on.

Teaser campaigns don't have to be subtle or contain a double meaning. The direct approach can work equally well. When we introduced a new product for a company that makes salt we sent out small bags of the new product and asked people to bring them to the meeting. That wasn't subtle at all. It told them exactly what to expect because imprinted on the bags were the words "Can the best really get better?" That was what the meeting was all about — the improvement of an established product and how the attendees, as salespeople, could capitalize on that improvement. On the other side of the bag was printed the original name of the product as well as the new name. Three short lines summarized the significant differences between the old and new products.

On the other hand, for the moving company whose salespeople couldn't handle selling in a corporate environment we sent a postcard that said only "$2+2=5$." In this case we wanted subtlety.

We wanted these salespeople to come to the meeting puzzled about the missing ingredient in their approach to selling.

All kinds of gimmicks, from 3-D glasses to keys to special locks, can be used in teaser campaigns. Once I distributed baseball cards containing pictures and information about people who were going to attend. The attendees had to find the person whose card they had. Since many of these people didn't know each other, this little game was an effective icebreaker.

Another way of using a teaser campaign to get people thinking is to combine fun and games with an audience questionnaire. Along with the "2 + 2 = 5" postcard we sent a questionnaire that asked such questions as "When was the last time you were in a corporate head office selling to a senior executive? How did you feel about it? What sort of problems did you encounter?" This served to let them know that the missing ingredient in the equation related to selling in corporate head offices.

Advertising is the art of making the potential consumer itchy enough about a product that he or she has to own it. It implies a question. Are you really satisfied with your car, with your brand of spaghetti sauce, with your bubble gum? The answer the marketer wants is no. Our new Chewy Peachy bubble gum is the best, so how could you be satisfied with anything else?

The same principle applies to internal advertising. Your meeting attendees are your target audience. They are the people to whom you are going to advertise. You want to make them itchy. You want them to ask questions. Am I really satisfied with my current level of activity? Are my campaign ideas effective? Am I satisfied with the sales I'm getting? Am I happy about the product? Does our company have a competitive advantage in the marketplace? The answer you probably want to these questions is "Yes — but I can do better."

To get that answer you need a message. There are only two things to know about a message. One is that the more words it contains, the less effective it is. The second is that the few words that you do use must be choice ones. A teaser can be a question, a call to action or an order, a title, or a statement.

For an accounting firm, I used the teaser "What counts?" For a telecommunications company, the teaser was "Prospects?" as part of a gold rush concept we had developed for the meeting. For a restaurant company that had a meeting with a sailing theme, our teaser was a call to action: "Steer the course."

A title is an effective way to raise curiosity. For a packaged goods company that had to sell to large supermarket chains, we used the theme, "A *key* chain."

Use a statement when you want the meeting attendees to know in advance that something is happening, can happen, will happen, or has happened. It's like staking out a position. "We can dream it...we can do it!" is a powerful example. For a manufacturer of cookware we used the theme "The future is now" to indicate that what people did now would affect the company for years to come.

In internal advertising you can either run a long campaign or do one big blast. Your choice depends on how much time you have. If time is short, then obviously you'll opt for a big blast. However, it's more effective to plan ahead and give yourself time for a longer campaign.

As you get closer and closer to the meeting, interest levels begin to rise naturally, whether or not you have a teaser campaign. People start to become curious approximately three weeks before the meeting. Some are looking forward to it. Some aren't, but even they are curious about what it's going to be like.

By starting a teaser campaign six weeks before a meeting, you can effectively double the amount of time in which you have to get people interested. The six-week period gives you a chance to take control of the mind of your audience before preconceived notions and assumptions set in. The teaser campaign lets you short-circuit that process.

A long campaign always has a better chance of penetrating people's minds and being remembered than a big blast. After all, we live in a world of big blasts. We get blasted every time we turn on the radio or television. To protect ourselves, we've become selective and we tune out most of what we hear. But a cleverly designed teaser campaign that's relevant to daily business life has a good chance of getting through.

The process of designing a message is largely the process of elimination. "Rise above the Rest" was fifteen paragraphs of writing before we boiled it down. Advertising copywriters will tell you they would be rich if they got paid for all the words they write when they're developing a campaign. What they get paid for is eliminating 99.9 percent of those words, condensing those pages and pages of thoughts into something concise and powerful that their audience understands.

I was peripherally involved in a meeting designed around the message "We are all going together into the future and the future looks great." I won't take responsibility for that message because it wasn't my choice. People didn't respond to it because it was too obvious. Their reaction was "That's corporate hype." A better message would have been a question such as "Is the future great?" or "A great future?"

Another one I didn't like was "Power." It was simple and it looked good but it didn't work. The audience was made up of engineers and the subject was the safety problems associated with nuclear reactors. "Safety" would have been a more pertinent message.

On another occasion, a meeting presented the message "Achieve wonderful things through quality." The problem was that this company's products had no quality whatsoever. Its message should have been "How do we achieve quality?"

The reason these messages were bad wasn't because the words were bad but because they didn't reflect the real problem that the company or group was facing. All too often some genius dreams up a message without doing the research necessary to ensure that it's relevant or realistic. The end result is a counterproductive meeting because it gets off to a bad start. Try turning around a herd of cattle that's pounding off in the wrong direction. It's part of the planning team's job to set them off in the right direction to begin with.

SELLING YOUR MESSAGE

With your planning team, you've designed your message, you know what you want to say, and you've conditioned your meeting attendees with a witty teaser campaign. Now your problem is selling your message. Even though you've attracted their interest, they don't have to buy what you're selling. To guarantee that they will buy it, you must do research — the single most powerful, and the least used, tool in meeting design. Research is asking questions and discovering the state of mind of your audience. That doesn't mean you are going to do exactly what the audience wants; they may not have any better idea than your planning group of how to attain the meeting's objectives. But it does mean integrating your objectives with the current state of mind of your audience. Don't make unwarranted assumptions about your audience. Don't design a meeting for an audience that doesn't exist.

Listening is probably the most effective of all sales techniques.

Good salespeople are always good listeners. They know how to ask the right questions and get the information that will identify areas of need to which they can sell.

RESEARCH YOUR AUDIENCE

In audience research, the planning team's aim is to get the information that will make the meeting beneficial and enjoyable for the audience and productive for your organization. Depending on the size of the potential audience, you should interview at least ten percent. The size of your sample will depend on how homogeneous the audience is. If they're all middle-aged salespeople with high school education and from the same geographical area, ten percent will do because their answers will be similar. If you only have ten people in your audience, talk to all of them.

Questionnaires are a valuable information-gathering tool. If you have access to a marketing research service or an experienced meeting consultant who has conducted audience research previously, enlist the aid of these professionals in designing your questionnaire. The most direct benefit of using outside resources is that the report you receive will be objective, unclouded by corporate or personal biases. If you don't have access to outside professionals, remember the following three points when designing your own questionnaire:

1. Your questionnaire should identify specific characteristics of your audience (e.g., age, gender, position, and seniority). This information will help you to fine-tune your event for the distinct groups attending it.
2. If at all possible, use no more than one question that calls for an essay-type answer. It is preferable to use multiple-choice questions or ones that can be answered with a yes/no response. Try to limit your questionnaires to no more than eight questions. People will more often take the time to respond to a short questionnaire than to a three-page monster.
3. Whenever possible, try to incorporate a quantifiable measure into your questionnaire (e.g., On a scale of 0 to 10, please indicate your desire for extra workshops in the evening; 0 indicates no desire and 10 indicates strong desire.). In this way you can identify trends and make your analysis less vulnerable to subjective interpretation.

If your questionnaire uncovers an interesting trend or an unexpected finding, don't hesitate to send out another questionnaire to another sample of people. If the results are replicated, the information is valid and should be acted on.

Also, restrict the number of questionnaires that you send out. We've distributed questionnaires to as many as two hundred people, which is probably the upper limit. Going through more than two hundred questionnaires is extremely time-consuming.

A final caution regarding questionnaires: always remember that questionnaires are only a tool and cannot replace your own understanding of your business and people. Nor can a questionnaire replace a face-to-face interview for some purposes.

Using questionnaires or personal interviews, find out whether the people who will attend the meeting are oriented toward empirical data, facts, things, numbers, or whether they are the type that love to interact with other people, to talk, laugh, listen, and learn. Your findings will determine many of your communications choices. Somebody once said it's the difference between an accountant and a preacher. The preacher is a people-person and the accountant is a numbers-person. Of course, that stereotype is often untrue. Many accountants are gregarious types while a glance at Sunday morning television reveals a definite numbers-orientation among certain preachers.

You need to be aware of the culture in which your attendees live, their age, education, their psychographics. Are they sports-minded or do they prefer the opera? Do they drink beer or twelve-year-old Scotch? Are they conservatives or liberals?

What are their expectations? What is their view of themselves? What do they think they deserve? If they think they deserve a lot, you'd better give them a lot. If you don't, you'll have some unhappy guests on your hands. My definition of a crowd is an unhappy group of people. If you want to deal with a crowd, ignore the individual and you'll get a crowd reaction.

You need to know how much knowledge and experience your audience brings to the meeting. Too much knowledge often produces skeptics and cynics who react as follows: "I know better. You can't tell me anything. You're manipulating me and I'm not going to accept that." If you're aware of these attitudes in advance, your team can do something about them.

Although I have been faced often with attendees who are cynical about any prospects for improvement in their organization's situation, I have never met a bunch quite like the engineers I interviewed as part of my research in designing training seminars that were to be part of an upcoming meeting. Some of them had been in the same company for more than twenty-five years and to the last person they said, "We simply don't believe that this organization's attitude about its people is moving into the twentieth century."

"What would make you believe it?" I asked.

"You can't make us believe the impossible," came the reply.

My research showed that five critical areas formed the foundation of these engineers' negative attitudes toward their employer. First were certain personnel policies, such as too many parking spaces reserved for senior management. Second were training policies, such as the company's refusal to pay for outside training. Third was a random vacation policy based on management assumptions and biases. Fourth was a hiring policy that seemed unfair and fifth was a lack of marketing sophistication in a market that was becoming increasingly competitive and sophisticated.

When I presented the senior managers with an agenda based on producing real changes in these five critical areas, they refused even to consider it. "Why bother to fix what has previously worked so well?" was their attitude. And it was true that the company had enjoyed great success based on the business of a small number of loyal clients obtained from the old-boy networking of the senior partners.

That attitude changed six months later, however, when a major account switched to a more aggressive firm. Management finally realized that it was time to get the staff engineers to drop their guard and open up their thinking by fully participating in a revitalization and reorganization of the company. We ran a three-day revitalization retreat to which the senior partners and representatives of each department were invited. The theme was "The Future Is Now." We dealt with every single aspect of the five problem areas and came away with an action plan covering forty pages. A professional facilitator I hired to run the meeting had to work so hard he lost several pounds but he succeeded in starting the company off on a return to productivity, a process that is continuing strongly to this day.

Understanding your audience is particularly important when you come to the point of making choices among the many kinds of media available. If your audience is visually oriented, audio-visuals may be more appropriate than reams of printed material.

For people who like to participate, there are interaction setups using telephones, videos or computers. We'll describe these in more detail later.

I designed a meeting for a company that was under severe competitive pressure. Its salespeople were complaining continuously about how tough things were. We looked for a medium that would illustrate that they were right, that indeed it was a jungle out there.

We wanted to tell them, "We know you're living in a competitive world and we're glad that your competition is tough. If it weren't, you would find it too easy and you wouldn't be as good as you are. Competition is good for the marketplace. Without competition, you'd have to do all of the selling. In fact, your competitors, by sensitizing the market, are doing some of the selling for you. In a monopoly market, people might lose interest in your product. Competition produces excitement and excitement produces buyers."

To get that message across, we chose the medium of sound. We turned out all the lights, leaving the room as dark as a cave except for tiny floor lights. Using those lights, we seated five hundred people. Then we turned the floor lights out and left the audience in the dark for thirty seconds while jungle sounds started to come out of the loudspeakers: a monkey, a macaw, an elephant, a lion. These sounds moved around the room to the front and suddenly on a screen the audience hadn't known was there, a gigantic visual appeared of a lion jumping out of the bush straight at the audience. A voice-over said, "It's a jungle out there" and started to explain the message.

This audience knew beforehand that the meeting would deal with competition but it didn't know what to expect. Shock tactics — darkness, strange sounds, and the dazzling visual — worked well. It made the point dramatically right from the start and convinced the salespeople that this was something important and that they had better pay attention. We were after effect and that's what we got. The lesson here is that communications are not just words: they are the way words and ideas are delivered.

ACT ON YOUR FINDINGS

What do you do when you've discovered the audience's needs? You do what a good salesperson does. If the salesperson finds that you need a ballpoint pen, does he or she try to sell you a lead pencil? Not if that person wants to remain in business.

Suppose your organization is concerned that certain practices are too expensive and it wants to address that problem in a meeting. Meanwhile, your research has told you that organization members themselves believe some of these practices are ineffective and should be reexamined with a view to changing them. Clearly, there is a mutuality of interest between the organization's concerns and those of the members.

You'll have a better chance of getting the cooperation you need if you address the members' needs in your message. "Make every dollar count" won't do the job. "Make every day count" will.

Look at your meeting as a win-win situation. You're finding out what your audience needs and you know what you want to achieve and how to achieve it. The end result should be an integration of their needs and your goal.

A client asked me to design a rest-and-relaxation meeting. I asked why and the answer was "Because these people work way too hard for us and we want to reward them, let them sit back, talk, and have some fun." That was a justifiable objective but I went ahead and did some audience research anyway. It turned out that the staff did need rest and relaxation. But they also wanted to learn a new technique or two, to become better at their jobs. The obvious solution was to blend the two needs into a combination that satisfied both client and audience.

In pursuing the sales approach it's important to avoid the salesperson's biggest mistake — not wanting to hear bad news. If someone tells you something you don't like, do something constructive about it. If you ignore something you don't want to hear, the meeting won't work.

That's what happened to an association of electronic equipment manufacturers that asked me to reenergize an annual convention for its members. Against the association's wishes, I insisted on the right to interview some of the previous attendees. I discovered that in the past the agenda had been so loaded and tightly packed that everyone was exhausted by the end. The attendees were treated as passive spectators. As a result, at least half the information was forgotten a few days later.

I redesigned the agenda to incorporate more breathing space and audience participation. However, the association's director rejected the revised agenda and the research that prompted it. "This is strictly a business meeting," she said. "Let them have fun on their own time."

They held the convention their own way. It was as if they were *trying* to ensure that their members retained no more than half the information presented to them. Why bother to hold such a terrible meeting at all?

REFLECT THE CORPORATE CULTURE

Marshall McLuhan was the most profound analyst of communications of our time. The essence of his philosophy boils down to the catch phrase "The medium is the message." It's also true that the meeting is the message. A meeting makes a statement about the organization that presents it. The meeting says, "This is who we are and what we have to offer and what we think of the people we've invited." If the meeting is shoddy, cheap, and disorganized, it says "Our company is shoddy, cheap, and disorganized and we don't think much of you either." Remember how you felt the last time you went to a movie that was heavily advertised as great entertainment and yet offered nothing in the way of a good story or interesting characters. People have the same negative reaction to bad meetings.

It's vital that your meeting reflect who you are as an organization. Each organization is different, has its own way of operating, and its own culture. A meeting must reflect that corporate persona. If you're an auditing firm and you operate in a strict, rigorous, by-the-book fashion, that personality should be evident in your meeting. It should be tightly disciplined and tightly scheduled because that's the kind of company you are.

Your meeting also reflects what your organization has to offer. Your organization is positioned in its sphere in a certain way and the meeting must reflect that positioning. Suppose a soft drink company presents itself as the premium pop manufacturer in the market. Everything it does, from the labels on its bottles to the uniforms on its drivers to the paint jobs on its trucks, should shout quality.

Now suppose this soft drink company decides to hold a meeting to bring management and staff in touch with market conditions. The decisions made on every element of that meeting must strictly reflect the dedication to quality that the company spends so much money talking about. As the planning team for that company, you can't use a second-rate hotel or decorate the meeting room with last year's outdated material.

If you do, your attendees will react in one of only two possible ways. Either, "We really are working for a quality company and

whoever put this meeting on made a mistake." Or, "The company is sending us the message that it is not a premium-quality
outfit, and it is lying when it says it is."

If your meeting is out of sync with your positioning, you are
delivering conflicting messages to your audience. The end result
is a mood of skepticism and cynicism.

Most important, your meeting should reflect what you as an
organization feel about your members. The truth, one hopes, is
that the members are important, a rich resource without whom
the organization couldn't do what it does. Many executives
mouth these platitudes but then they present meetings that
demonstrate they don't really believe them.

The meetings are dull and dictatorial with a minimum of
audience participation. They are counterproductive because
they are telling the members, "This is what you *need* to know.
This is what you should do now. Follow orders. Don't think."
The single biggest complaint I hear from attendees is "I was
treated like a fool." A meeting that provokes such a response is a
disaster, and the way to avoid that disaster is to know your
audience.

REPEATING THE MESSAGE

It is not enough to simply give people information and tell them
to memorize it. You have to make them think about the information and use it. If one of the goals of your meeting is to present a
new sales manual, set up workshops in which individuals actually play out the different situations dealt with in the manual.
Only about thirty percent of your time should be devoted to
dispensing information. The rest of the time should be spent in
workshops or seminars where use of that information is demonstrated.

Why thirty percent? Because presenting the information is the
easy part. It takes much longer for it to sink in to the point where
people are capable of integrating it into a daily routine. Before
the meeting ends, your message should be reviewed at least
twice, actually used at least once, and thought about continuously. Only through such reinforcement can anything of long-
term significance happen.

Advertisers have long recognized the necessity of this kind of
repetition and repeat their messages many times in many different ways. Eventually, the message develops momentum and
takes on a life of its own. Your goal is the same. By using different

media — audio-visuals, speeches, workbooks, workshops — you provide different angles on the same information. And the more different angles you provide, the more likely it is that the audience will remember your message in the months following.

Nothing works as well as tie-ins. Relate what you're trying to teach someone to what the person already knows. If you have to describe a kiwi fruit to someone who's never seen one, you'll compare the size, shape, feel, and taste of it to other fruits that the person does know. Here's where all of the research that you did before the meeting pays off, because you make use of your audience's background, experience, jargon, and knowledge by relating all of that to your message. You give them new information but you give it to them in terms of what they already know.

I organized a meeting to present a new product to a group of packaged-goods salespeople. The typical marketing presentation uses a lot of facts and figures presented through charts, graphs, and overheads. But we decided to try to present this product in terms of its impact on the trade buyers who make the buying decisions for chain stores and supermarkets. We said to the salespeople, "This product is so good it will change the trade buyers' perception of all your products."

We showed videos portraying before-and-after situations. The before video had a man, who was offscreen, talking to a buyer. He was pitching the new product to the buyer and the buyer was resisting, saying he didn't believe the pitch about the new, improved quality and the better packaging graphics. It was the basic "show-me" attitude.

At that point, we stopped the video and started talking about why the buyer was resisting and how you could describe the product in a way that would convince the buyer of its merits. Led by the sales manager, we developed some techniques for achieving this.

Later, we showed the after video, in which the sales manager put into practice everything we had discussed after the first one. This time the trade buyer was convinced. It was a successful method for conveying a message because it made use of the attendees' own experience and presented a situation with which they could identify totally.

Knowing how much message to give your people and in what ways is a bit like knowing how quickly or slowly you can drive on a highway without getting stopped by a policeman. It's a matter of feel. If you feel that your attendees are the type who will get a message quickly through the use of a strong visual medium then you might need to dedicate only about five percent of the meeting to strong visual presentations. The rest of the time could be left for seminars, workshops, open sessions, forums, or panel discussions.

You should consider using audio-visual media when you have finished one section of the meeting and are about to start a new section. For instance, you have just dealt with last year's sales achievements and are about to start looking at this year's projection versus the actual results to date. A strong visual impact might well be appropriate at that time.

You could just show the numbers but that won't give you a powerful impact. At one meeting, I used a variation that worked well. We interviewed major customers of the company on videotape, asking them why they spent more or less on our company's products than had been projected. The actual expenditures, compared to the projections, were shown on the screen while the client was talking.

It's up to you to decide whether your situation requires that kind of treatment. As I said above, it's really a question of feel. Meeting planning is an art, not a science.

Remember that too much use of strong visuals will numb your audience. This is the television age and people are exposed constantly to powerful visuals of war, suffering, pain, and joy. It's difficult to compete with that.

If your audience is a group of accountants whose prime orientation is toward the logical, verbal, and analytical rather than the visual, then you won't want to fill your meeting with slides, films, and videotapes because they might not respond. Salespeople, on the other hand, usually respond well to audio-visuals that involve people rather than things. If you are doing a new product introduction to a group of salespeople, it's a good idea to give them a strong dose of audio-visuals portraying people using the product.

You want to introduce your message at the start of the meeting and you probably should reinforce it when a break occurs for coffee or lunch, so that they leave with the message on their minds. The end of the day and whenever you summarize or recap are other good times to reinforce what has been said. Of course, there are many other opportunities. It all depends on the audience and your understanding of it.

WORKSHOPS, PANELS, AND SEMINARS

Workshops, panels, and seminars are the most highly interactive and participative of all types of communications and therefore require a large amount of input. The more information that you can feed the participants beforehand, the more interactive such sessions will be. Therefore, such activities should follow a plenary or general information session. Give your participants something to talk about and they will talk.

Well-trained facilitators for these sessions are a rare breed. This is a demanding exercise that calls for well-honed listening skills, great patience, and the ability to keep the sessions focused yet flexible — as well as a sense of humor. If you have contact with a consulting firm, ask for their recommendations. Or you could contact the American Management Association (usually listed under AMA in the white pages of the phone book) or the American Society for Training and Development. Several branches of the ASTD are located in Canada. Check the white pages of the phone book for their listings under, for example, "Manitoba Society for Training and Development," or "Training and Development Society of British Columbia." These groups can often find top-quality workshop or seminar leaders, complete with references.

Since it takes several years of hands-on experience to produce a mature and effective facilitator who also has strong people-skills, do not attempt to train a junior or to drop a senior executive into this caldron of stress. Expertise in the subject area is critical, but by itself it's not enough.

Workshops and seminars featuring hands-on exercises and feedback are an important part of the reinforcement process. Like the meeting itself, a workshop must have a clearly defined purpose as well as a skilled facilitator. Without one, it has no direction and that's no good because a workshop is supposed to result in the solution to a specific problem.

Perhaps you need a finished action plan to install a new piece of plant equipment. That's the sort of problem that's well suited to solution in a workshop. First, identify the parts of the problem that must be dealt with: specifications, space, delivery schedules, etc. Set a time limit on decision making; for example, allow ten minutes to make a decision on each item. Set decision-making rules; for example, a fifty-one percent majority is decisive. And decide in advance how you will judge when the desired outcome has been achieved; in this case, it's when you have a completed action plan containing clear and precise decisions on all aspects of the installation.

Question-and-answer sessions can be very touchy. Unless the people on your panel are prepared to answer all questions, these sessions can degenerate as follows:

"We won't answer that question now. It's not appropriate."

"Why isn't it appropriate?"

"Well, we just don't want to answer it now."

"Why not?"

"It's not appropriate."

If someone brings up a question that you can't answer, then say so, and promise to get the information. If you're not willing to answer all questions, then preface the question-and-answer session by saying, "We will not answer any questions on the following items." If people are prepared to accept that, fine. If they aren't, then it's best to skip the session.

An open panel allows non-experts to ask questions of, and provide feedback to, a select group of experts. The expert panel should contain between three and six people. They present their views on the issues under discussion and raise questions about areas that aren't clear. This last part is important because the experts don't have all the answers. They may well be depending on the audience to provide some of those answers.

After the experts have spoken, the audience has a chance to have its say in any form it wants — questions, statements, opinions, arguments. You need a moderator and a secretary who will record what is said, as instructed by the moderator. It's important that the moderator cull only the useful material from the session for the permanent record.

An open panel works best when it's sandwiched between an information session and a question-and-answer session. Suppose you have shown an audio-visual presentation about a new Outreach program for the community. You follow that up with an open panel on the pros and cons of the new program. Finally, the question-and-answer session gives people a chance to speak their minds on what they've just seen and heard.

THE ART OF LISTENING

Transmitting information isn't just telling people things. It's also listening. When I train individuals in the art of moderating workshops, I try to get them to develop the art of listening. To listen well, you must learn to concentrate. One exercise I use when training people in the art of listening is a game called "Carry on the Story." Two people sit facing each other and one of them starts to tell a story. After a few sentences, the first person will stop and the other person has to continue as if it was still the first person telling the story.

Suppose the first person is talking about his dog — where he got him, the kind he is, his habits and idiosyncracies. Then he stops suddenly, and the other person carries on. But the second person is not talking about her own dog — she's talking about the first person's dog, as if that first person were still speaking. It can't be done convincingly unless she was listening extremely closely to the first person. It's a tough exercise and one that takes a lot of practice but it's an effective way to build listening skills.

Surprisingly, another method is to study speed-reading. In speed-reading, we train our eyes to search for whole concepts rather than individual words. In so doing, we stop vocalizing those words mentally, thereby increasing our rate of absorption of written material. Speed-reading trains our visual sense. Seeing well is an important part of effective listening. The good listener watches how people react, how their bodies move, the expressions on their faces, how they fidget with their hands.

Part of the art of listening is insisting that the participants express themselves clearly. If you don't understand what someone has said, ask him what he means. Then say something like, "If I understand you correctly, what you are saying is...." Only when that understanding is reached can you proceed to the next point. The long-term usefulness of any newly acquired knowledge or skill depends on how well it was first understood. That is why active listening plays such an important role in producing the change you're after.

Problem Solving

An important part of producing long-term results is the resolution of problems. The greater the problem, the more lasting the effects of its resolution are likely to be. Some meetings are specifically designed to address an issue and solve a problem. The planning team has to identify the problem and issue in a way that everyone will understand.

Ask fifty people about an issue and you'll probably get fifty different answers. But if fifty people are coming to a meeting to solve a problem, you can't afford to have them see that problem in fifty different ways. They may have different views on how to solve it but they have to agree at the start on what the problem is.

To solve a problem, you need everybody's contribution. How do you encourage people to contribute? One technique is personalization. You know the attendees' names, histories, and areas of expertise. Suppose Joe Brown is a loner. You know that he's a specialist in management information systems (MIS) and your problem has a major MIS component. You can encourage Joe to lend his expertise to solving the problem. By doing so you give him a chance to be a hero: it gives meaning to his career and his very existence to be seen as making a great contribution. Identify Joe by name, state what sort of contribution he can make, stress how important this contribution will be, and alleviate any fears of embarrassment that he may have. "Joe, it's very important at this stage just to come up with some ideas. We'll be able to work with any ideas we can get. What do you say?"

An agenda is a key tool in the problem-solving process. Some people like to throw out a bunch of ideas and toss them around. But that can result in a disorganized meeting with no focus. It's better to allot a certain amount of time to each aspect of a problem. The agenda must reflect a logic that the audience will understand.

Suppose your association has a membership problem involving promotion, advertising, and fees. Your agenda for the meeting should reflect the chronological and critical priorities of those areas. If financial or fee-related problems are playing the major role in the overall problem, you start there and spend the most time on that problem. It seems logical to put advertising after the discussion of financial matters because fees must be attractive before they can be advertised. Therefore, advertising is handled next and it's related to what has already been said about fees and to what will be said on promotions. The reason for sticking to an agenda is that it represents a logical approach to a problem.

Solving a problem is only the first part of the battle. The next step is to do something about it. I call that "action planning." You must come out of the meeting with accurate minutes that clearly describe the problem, the possible solutions, the responsibilities of the people involved, and a schedule. The minutes should be posted for all to see. Without an action plan, what seemed like a productive, problem-solving meeting will fail to produce results.

The only reliable way to produce significant change is to get people involved. The best time to get them involved is at the beginning and an action plan provides immediate involvement. As the project proceeds, the action plan works as a road map.

Maximizing Learning Ability

If one of the objectives of your meeting is to educate your attendees on a particular subject you must understand how people learn. Learning takes place on a curve that at first is steep but gradually flattens out as less and less learning takes place. Creating bridges between different events in the meeting helps to keep the learning curve as steep as possible for as long as possible.

There's a technique called "Venning" (after a mathematician named Venn, who invented the Venn diagram) that is used to illustrate what two elements have in common (see Figure 3-1). Two circles intersect and the area of intersection is the area in common. The meeting planner should strive to achieve areas of commonality among the different elements of your meeting. If,

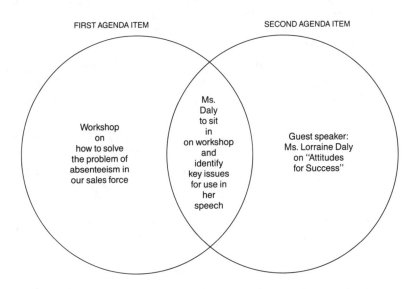

FIRST AGENDA ITEM   SECOND AGENDA ITEM

Workshop on how to solve the problem of absenteeism in our sales force

Ms. Daly to sit in on workshop and identify key issues for use in her speech

Guest speaker: Ms. Lorraine Daly on "Attitudes for Success"

Figure 3-1 Venn Diagram

for example, a workshop is scheduled that deals with a problem-solving situation and the next event is a guest speaker, a bridge is needed between the two of them.

Suppose that the workshop was dealing with the problem of absenteeism in the sales force. You know the workshop will come up with something, but you've no way of predicting what. Meanwhile, you've scheduled a guest speaker for after the workshop and you know she's going to be talking about attitudes.

To create the necessary bridge, ask the guest speaker to sit in on the workshop. Explain that the workshop is going to be dealing with absenteeism and suggest that she link that issue to what she will be talking about in her speech. This creates a sense among the audience that one thing flows naturally into another.

Suppose you're introducing a new product with six distinct features and you want to make sure your salespeople learn this product inside out. The following sets out how you can adjust the information you are dispensing to take advantage of the learning curve.

1. Define your desired end result precisely: your salespeople must have a thorough knowledge of the new product and all its six features.
2. Start with a powerful and concise introduction. You might create an acronym using the first letters of the features of the product, as in SUREST: S for strong, U for unbreakable, R for reliable, E for energy-saving, S for serviceable and T for trustworthy.
3. Break the different elements into related clusters. Perhaps this product is small and is sold in single units. These two characteristics can be related and discussed at the same time.
4. Deal with each feature individually and in depth. Use visual aids. Compare it to other similar products.
5. It's now late in the learning curve and you want people to start using the information and feeding it back. Ask them to demonstrate what they've learned. Perhaps one of the features of the product is that it has a tough outer coating. How would they use that feature to help sell the product to trade buyers?
6. Offer a general summary, once again using the acronym, showing how the six features relate to each other and discussing how the information can be applied.

Highways are marked by signposts that tell us how far we've come on our journey and how far we've got to go. Meetings have signposts too. I once organized a meeting for a manufacturer of video equipment. The aim of the meeting was to teach people about the ways in which a series of new products could be used. After one day, we ran a video game that presented a series of questions. The attendees could answer some of them based on what they had already learned. Others could not be answered until the following day. This exercise allowed them to understand where they were in the learning process and to know where they would be when that process was complete.

A workbook or a computer game can be designed to work as a signpost. So can an open panel discussion. You can tell the panel experts in advance that certain information has been covered so far and ask them to summarize it in their talks and to indicate how much more must be learned.

It's up to you to decide when it's time to erect a signpost in your meeting. If people have been through several sessions dealing with six or seven different items, perhaps it's time. Summarizing what's happened and pointing to what's still to come helps people organize the new information. It's an important aid to the learning process and a way of ensuring that what is learned is remembered and has an an impact long after the meeting is over.

Concentrating on Motivation

Motivation is the most poorly understood objective in meeting design. Millions of dollars are spent on so-called motivational meetings with highly charged keynote addresses, powerful messages, rallies, war cries and slogans. Yet whether any of this really succeeds in motivating anybody is rarely measured or tested.

The key to motivation is identification of what means the most to the attendees. This can then be used to spur them on to better performance. However, this identification process is often difficult because not everyone shares the same values.

Suppose an employee is faced with being fired if he doesn't do something. That threat doesn't automatically guarantee that he'll do it. Some people hate their jobs and would love to escape from them. By threatening an employee with "firing" you might inadvertently have offered him a good reason for not behaving as you want.

The first rule of motivation, then, is this: Don't assume that your target group shares your values. The corollary to this rule is that you need to know what the target group really does value. There are several ways of finding out.

The most obvious is simply to consider what has turned your audience on in the past. Once I had to choose between two motivational speakers. One was an industry expert and award-winning salesman in his field. The other was a mountain climber who had been part of a team that scaled Mount Everest. Our research revealed that the client's audience had never responded well to industry experts and that it was looking for "something different." We went with the mountain climber and he was a big success.

Another clue is current behavior that can be used to reinforce new behavior. I was asked to find a way to improve the functioning of middle-management meetings in a small engineering firm. The problem was that these Monday morning meetings took too long and produced too little. We talked to the people who attended the meetings and found that most of the real decisions were made after work at the local watering hole. All the middle managers looked forward to what they euphemistically called the "Bible Club."

I suggested a new approach. Instead of holding the meetings on Monday morning, move them to Friday afternoon, when no one would be in a mood to waste time. If the attendees achieved a predetermined set of objectives, they would be treated to one beer each at the Bible Club, compliments of the company. This system worked so well that the company gave the bar special beer mugs bearing the name of each club member.

Some motivational problems are the result of a long sequence of events. During the planning of a training seminar for a sales meeting, the sales manager indicated concern that the seminar might be too tightly organized. He had created a system for his salespeople in order to minimize their paperwork and their need to check things with him. But they were complaining that it was causing them more work. He was worried that the seminar would aggravate the situation.

The manager thought his staff was ungrateful but I suggested that they might actually be saying that they wanted more attention from him. We decided that *he* would give the seminar rather than an outside trainer, and that he would follow up by spending some individual time with each member of his staff. The results were improved attitudes and higher productivity.

You are trying to motivate people to achieve something but if that task seems too large they will refuse to be motivated. I designed a meeting for the salespeople of a company that had gone through a terrible time because of a serious environmental problem with its flagship product. They were down and looking to get up. That desire to feel good again had been correctly identified as a key motivator by the company, which had also defined sales objectives that it considered to be tough but achievable.

In planning the meeting, we incorporated a flood of good news forecasts and upbeat positive thinking sessions into the agenda. But when we tried out some material on a sample of the attendees, we got a negative reaction. The sales objectives struck them as much too ambitious.

We responded by restating the same objectives in terms of quarterly results rather than annual ones, and measured them in tonnages rather than dollar volumes. During the meeting, the attendees reacted enthusiastically and subsequently the company's sales objectives were achieved. The lesson is simply that it's often easier to motivate people to achieve a series of smaller goals rather than one big one.

Understanding the Interaction

Whether your meeting is called to transmit information, solve problems, teach new skills, motivate your people, or any combination of these purposes, you must understand the ways people interact in a group situation if you are to achieve your goals. By harnessing the power of group dynamics, capitalizing on the strength of cooperative and competitive events, and working within the inevitable hierarchies, you can help to increase your chances of success.

EFFECTIVE USE OF GROUP DYNAMICS

A group is a constantly changing phenomenon. The interplay and interaction of people in a group comprise what we call "group dynamics." There are two kinds of behavior within groups: individual behavior and group behavior. People don't stop being individuals just because they're thrown together in a large group; each person continues to act separately from the rest. But there is also group behavior, which is common to every-one in a group and which is the only behavior with which you can actually work. Group behavior is your tool for creating sig-nificant change. You can't design a meeting for each individual personality. You can, however, design it for a group of people that share some characteristics.

In attempting to modify group behavior, however, it's impor-tant to remember that a group response is made up of many individual responses, each of them different. You can look at the problem of managing a group of people in two ways. The first is gross management — getting them all moved more or less in the same direction and motivated in the same way at the same time. The other, which I prefer, is addressing each individual in a common way. In other words, I try to present the same informa-tion to many different people in the hope that, while each of them will absorb different things, they will arrive at a consensus when working together.

A consensus is a powerful thing. It implies commitment and that produces change that lasts. The *Declaration of Indepen-dence*, for example, was formulated through a consensus and subsequently has taken on great symbolic power.

Because group response is the sum of many individual responses, let's discuss individual behavior in a bit more detail. One of the most important characteristics of individual behavior is that it is modeled on the behavior of others. If everyone in the office is wearing a thin tie, then most people judge that to be "right" behavior. They go out and buy themselves thin ties.

The same dynamic works in a meeting. If one person shows up in a sports shirt the first day, and he's the only one wearing a sports shirt, it's a sure bet that on the second day he'll be dressed like everyone else. This sort of conformity is probably not what you are looking for in your people. I use it only as an example of how change can begin. The first step a person takes in a new direction is what sets him or her up for long-term significant change. The first step is the key that opens the door.

Another aspect of individual behavior is the "fight or flight reaction." Some people are apprehensive about being part of a large group. Either they want to get away from it, a flight reac-tion, or they get aggressive, a fight reaction. The first type of person stays on the fringes of the proceedings, and tries not to become involved. The other behaves in a domineering way.

In order to maintain control of the meeting, you must be

aware of, and watch for, these reactions. You also must understand that for most people, strange as it may seem, meetings are a form of isolation. A person leaves home and family, job, and daily routine, and goes to a strange place. As a result his or her behavior changes. The person does things he or she would never do at home. Bill, normally a sober type, stays up all night at conventions and gets drunk. Harry, a loner back at the office, joins in all kinds of group activities. Elaine, usually a wallflower at parties, suddenly dances up a storm. Being away from normal routines usually changes people's behavior.

Any change in behavior parallels a similar change in a person's mental state. When someone is jolted out of everyday reality, he or she is more susceptible to fundamental change. Cults are able to brainwash their victims through a rapid, disorienting change in their environment that sets up a psychological dependence on a new truth. The effect of a meeting is a comparable, although much milder and more benign, form of significant change.

The psychology of teenage gangs isn't unlike that of groups of adults attending a business meeting. Both are groups and groups are more willing to be led than individuals. They look for a leader. They are willing to go with the flow. Their behavior is often irrational. A momentum of laughter or some other strong reaction can sweep through a group, threatening your control.

Cynicism and skepticism are two such reactions. Cynicism is the self-defense mechanism of the weak individual. Isolated in a meeting and feeling threatened as a result, he or she retreats more strongly than ever into cynicism. The skeptic, on the other hand, has a "show-me" attitude that says, "This is what I think, either prove to me that I'm wrong or show me that you're right." Skepticism is a form of question, while cynicism is a form of answer. Since you want people to arrive with questions, not answers, skepticism is by far the better attitude because you can do something about it. If you are able to convince a skeptic, you have the chance to make a permanent change in his or her thinking. Cynics, on the other hand, are highly committed to their current mind-set. It's hard for them to accept what you're offering as a better alternative.

If you can generate a common emotional level in the group, you can strengthen the attachment the individuals will have to the message you are presenting. If you can achieve a group feeling among the attendees, you are well on your way to leading them to the decisions and commitments you want.

Every meeting, and every group within that meeting, has a focus. It revolves either around your point or something of its own choosing. The best way to ensure that the meeting is focused where you want it to be is to make that focus very strong. This can be achieved by a step-by-step approach to meeting design:

1. Find out your audience's "hot spot." If the hot spot is credibility — they don't believe what the organization is telling them — bring in credible witnesses. If your audience is a group of fund raisers, an experienced and accomplished fund raiser could provide the focus.
2. "Key in" your message. This is a polite way of saying cut the crap. Eliminate anything extraneous to the essential message.
3. Put the message in context. The more starkly you can contrast it to something else, the more strongly the message will stand out. And by relating it to other items as part of a larger issue, the importance of your message grows in stature.
4. Enhance the message. Use music, visuals, or hands-on displays. Let everyone experience the message with all their senses.
5. Create a symbolic representation of the message. People remember symbols better than abstract concepts. I ran a meeting on quality and our logo was a Q wrapped around itself in a striking and beautiful way. Every time people looked at it, they remembered the message.
6. Give your audience plenty of opportunity for feedback. Let them respond to the focus of the meeting and perform some activity related to what they are hearing.

Focusing is an important tool for creating long-term change because you can return over and over again to the focus point. Focus keeps everything in your meeting moving in the right direction.

Like a moving stream, a meeting has eddies and backwaters. The backwaters are the quiet, uninvolved people. The eddies are the groups of people who are interacting intensely among themselves. Often, they aren't focused.

If a small group of people is beginning to form a clique — playing cards all evening and constantly sticking together during the day — then you've got an eddy. The focus of that eddy is probably not the message of the meeting. Most meeting planners say, "Well, it will take care of itself." That's a recipe for losing control of your meeting. I'm not suggesting that you try to break these cliques up. But you have to listen to what these people are saying and determine whether their focus is similar to yours and then refocus them if necessary.

If the card game is going on in the evening or during a rest break, that's the cardplayers' business. If it's happening during prime meeting time, it's your business as well. You have to give them an incentive to stop playing cards and get involved in the meeting. If the boss comes up and says, "Get in that conference room or you're fired," they will have a strong incentive to stop playing cards, but it will do little to encourage a productive meeting. A better approach is to replace what they are doing with something of more value.

I ran a meeting for the operations people of a manufacturing company. When a group of card fiends were ignoring the meeting, I went up to them and said, "You guys are always bitching about how the marketing guys never know what's going on. Well, tonight we are putting together presentation teams of operations guys. They are going to be given marketing problems and they are going to have to solve those problems from a marketing point of view. Tomorrow they're going to present their work and the best team will get a hundred bucks."

I never saw people get up from a card table so fast. They were up until 3 a.m. working on their problem and they won the hundred dollars. Responding to such an incentive can be the beginning of a continuing involvement that ultimately leads to the kind of significant change I've been talking about.

Another technique is to trade attention to business at the meeting for future benefits. I ran a meeting in Florida for a publishing company. We were running into a lot of resistance from a group that was interested only in playing golf and refused to get involved in the meeting. We bribed them. We gave them a choice among several optional activities in the meeting and said that if they chose one we would take them to one of the best golf courses in Florida for two rounds of golf. They snapped up the offer and got down to work.

We continued to take advantage of their interest in golf throughout the following year by offering memberships in a top golf club for the best contributions to marketing operations. The original seed of involvement planted in the meeting grew into long-range, significant results.

Not only do individuals interact within groups, but smaller groups interact within larger groups. Break people up into teams, give each team a name and a series of contests in which to compete, and the competitive instinct comes to the surface. People are always seeking identity and you can provide it. The truism that there is safety in numbers applies here. We feel a lot better and more ready to participate when surrounded by friendly associates. Every group also seeks an opinion leader. It is important to remember this when presenting your message to your groups.

Let's take a situation that's common to many companies. You want your administration people to understand the problems that your operations people face when trying to meet production schedules. At the same time, you want your operations people to understand the pressure your administration is under when they try to make sure that follow-up service is satisfactory.

Take your two groups and assign each a case study. The administrative people get an operational one — for example, how to double production in two weeks. Meanwhile, the operations people have to grapple with the problem of how to produce a one hundred-page user's manual in two weeks.

An operations person and an administrative person are guests in each other's group. They are there to provide realistic guidance as people work out an unfamiliar problem. Finally, the two groups present their solutions to each other, with comment and criticism flowing back and forth. Both now know something that neither did before — what life is like in someone else's shoes. That usually produces a changed attitude, with long-term benefits for everyone.

Another element of group dynamics is intimate behavior. Some individuals choose to have one intimate friend throughout the meeting with whom they will share all sorts of activities. They prefer a one-to-one situation. I suggest that you give them an opportunity to work as part of a twosome if they feel they will work more effectively that way. When selecting teams, try to make sure that these twosomes get on the same team. Every positive and comforting experience digs a furrow into your attendee's mind and feelings, into which you can plant the seeds of long-term change.

The Stimulation of Competition and Cooperation

A meeting should have a balance between competition and cooperation. To design a cooperative event, your first step is to identify an issue that is important to everyone. For example, many companies and some non-profit and political organizations use incentive programs to stimulate their salespeople or membership and fund-raising people. This could be the issue.

Secondly, you state a problem. Should incentives be awarded to individuals or to groups? What should be the time frame — a month, a quarter, or a year? Should the rewards be in the form of cash, or prizes such as travel? If you don't obtain the required points in an incentive period, should you be able to carry some of your points over?

Thirdly, get all the different groups working on the different aspects of the problem. Finally you bring them together to enunciate a comprehensive solution to the entire problem. The final result is a solid sense of cooperation and forward movement. Cooperation can become habit-forming. It worked well once and people will want to continue to use it long after the meeting is over.

Most successful meetings produce significant change by carrying people through a whole series of competitive and cooperative ventures that reinforce the message by providing the same theme under different circumstances. Suppose you are in an industry that has only a few major players, for example, paging systems. The theme of your meeting is "Be the Very Best."

You could provide two sets of activities. The first would concentrate on the special production processes involved in producing paging devices — research and development, signal distribution, networking systems, and so on. Those involved in each area would compete with each other on the importance scale; they would have to argue why their area is the most indispensable to the success of the company. The next set of activities would be an idea-generating session on how each area could boost the company's competitive advantage.

The two sets of activities complement each other. In the first, each division has to justify its own existence in a competitive fashion. In the second, everybody comes together to search cooperatively for ways to bolster the company as a whole.

The mixture of competition and cooperation enriches the learning experience. However, don't forget that competitive events produce losers as well as winners. Your participants are going to experience a fear of failure and for that reason, too many competitive events can cause undue mental stress. Because you don't want the meeting to be a stressful experience for the attendees, I suggest a 60:40 ratio between cooperation and competitiveness, respectively.

The following are some ways to design cooperative experiences into your meeting.

- Start before the meeting by doing research to uncover commonly held beliefs and concerns.
- Analyze the issues down to their smallest discrete parts.
- Identify ways of dealing with each part of each problem.
- List the parts in order of importance.
- Produce a schedule based on these priorities.
- Assign responsibilities for the different tasks.
- Assign an overall project coordinator.
- Assign a secretary to handle recording and monitoring.

Suppose, in doing your research, you've found a widespread belief in your organization that communications are a problem area. Further research indicated that both internal and external communications are problematic. Probing further, you found that internal communications problems related to raises: people were displeased that they never knew when they would get raises and how much they could count on getting. The external problem turned out to be that clients were not being adequately informed about after-sale service.

On the issue of raises, it is decided that the way to deal with it is to inform staff of the timing and amount of raises three weeks in advance of the actual raises. On the issue of after-sale service, the task is to set a time limit within which clients will receive information.

You then think about which of these is most important and decide it's the issue of customer service. Responsibility for it is shared among the accounting office and the sales and service people. A coordinator, probably one of your senior executives, is chosen.

A similar process is followed for the other problem and you set up open sessions and workshops as necessary to grapple with the two problems. You know exactly what you're trying to achieve and the responsibilities have been assigned. That's a recipe for a fruitful meeting using teamwork.

The purpose is so clear that people find themselves drawn to the project. They feel good about themselves and what they are doing. That sort of feeling is what produces the momentum for long-term change.

Contending with Hierarchies

Interactions between individuals are always hierarchical. Whenever a group gets together, a pecking order is established. Age, experience, gender, wealth, manners, behavior, and social status all come into play. As individuals come together in a meeting, some will defer and others will assume major status. One of the reasons we do audience research is to find out what proportion of our audience will be leaders and what proportion will be followers. If it's a convention of professionals such as lawyers or doctors, for example, you might have a meeting full of chiefs with very few Indians because these professionals tend to be independent types. You have to design the meeting accordingly.

How could you cope with a too-many-chiefs situation? If you have done your research, you can identify key group issues that are common to everybody. Next, you separate those issues into distinct areas; for example, broad topics such as how to design a common data base for all professional uses and narrow issues such as how to deal with professionals using advertising to reach the general public. Third, you hold special workshops in which people work individually on the narrow issue and then come together to share and analyze each other's efforts. Finally, you hold a group brainstorm to address the broad issue of the professional information systems.

This design allows the "chiefs" to start out as individuals but it brings them together at the end. It's a design that allows the hierarchical nature of teaming to work for you to produce an atmosphere in which behavioral change can take root.

Careful meeting design is what gets people involved and involvement is what leads to significant change. If people have good experiences at a meeting, they will want to get involved in subsequent meetings in the expectation that those too will be satisfying. Your attendees will then present you with a challenge: "Let's have another great meeting like last year's, only let's make it even better." That's the challenge every good meeting team actively seeks.

4

THE AGENDA

The agenda is the blueprint that will turn your meeting design into reality. A good agenda is like a racetrack in that it directs the power of the "horses" — the different elements of your meeting — in a definite direction. If an agenda is inadequately designed, it is more like an open field and those elements will run all over the place to no purpose.

Mirror-Image Agenda

There are many different agenda layouts but most are variations or combinations of several basic types. The first type is the balanced or mirror-image agenda. This comprises a full or half-day itinerary that is repeated, but in reverse. For example, the first half-day is as follows.

1. Opening ceremonies
2. Welcoming addresses
3. "Message" audio-visual
4. Keynote speaker
5. Refreshment break
6. General session

That layout is then duplicated in reverse order during the next half day.

1. General session (continued)
2. Refreshment break
3. Specific-topic speaker
4. "Message" audio-visual
5. Closing remarks
6. Finale

The second half does not simply repeat or feed back word for word everything that went before. Rather, it reverses the format using different information or materials. It's a bit like running up a scale on a piano and then going back down. The familiar feeling of the second half helps to reinforce learning and the message.

Agenda formats of this type are best used when the most important events occur in the middle of the meeting. I used a mirror-image agenda like the one above for a clothing manufacturer that wanted to introduce a new production system into its plants. The center of the meeting was an open forum at which employees could discuss the system and ask questions about it. The rest of the meeting reinforced the key points at least twice — first leading up to the open forum, and then leading away from it. It worked perfectly.

Sandwich Agenda

Another layout is the contraction/expansion or sandwich approach. In this layout, the agenda is divided into three separate blocks. The first is a short, structured, intense session that presents and treats specific, clearly defined issues. The middle or main body session is open, longer, and more unstructured; it deals with concepts, feelings, ideas, and opinions. The final block, like the first, is short, structured, and intense; it merges the results of both blocks into a concise and action-oriented wrap-up.

A sandwich agenda should have long, well-defined breaks between each block but no breaks during a block except for short ones for refreshments. The following is a sample agenda.

First block: 1. Audio visual that highlights the issues
 2. Five-minute presentation of key points by a senior executive
 3. Definition of specific objectives
 4. Listing of available resources

One-hour break

Main body: 1. Breakout workshops
 2. General discussion and think time
 3. Presentation of results

End of first day

Third block: 1. Presentation of action-plan formats
                2. Selection of action items
                3. Review of objectives and solutions
                4. Closing remarks

The main body is usually at least three times as long as the two other blocks. It's important that it contain plenty of free-for-all discussion time. The contrast between the intensity of the first and final sessions with the more free-floating atmosphere of the middle session lends a feeling of excitement to the event.

The sandwich agenda is great for networking in a resort setting. I have used the same format for four successive resort meetings for the same client and it has built up a tradition of success. This meeting layout encourages people who might in other arrangements remain uninvolved to get down to business. At the same time, it preserves an atmosphere of rest and relaxation, which is an important part of an event held at a resort.

Parallel Agenda

Yet another meeting layout is the parallel agenda. This is really two agendas that run separately until they meet in a joint closing session, as shown in the following.

Block A	Block B
1. Opening remarks	1. Opening remarks
2. Audio-visual	2. Audio-visual
3. Executive presentation	3. Keynote speaker
4. Keynote speaker	4. Executive presentation
5. Break	5. Break
6. Workshops	6. Training session
7. Training session	7. Workshops

Block C
1. General review
2. Group/workshop presentations
3. Panel discussion
4. Wrap-up remarks
5. Closing dinner

The parallel agenda is good for working on internal problems, such as misunderstandings between membership-contact people and purely administrative or clerical staff of a large association with branches across the country. You might have the administrative or clerical people study the day-to-day problems faced by their membership-contact colleagues while the other agenda would do the opposite. Consciousness-raising for both groups takes place simultaneously.

The two agendas should have a lot in common. For example, the keynote speaker should be the same for both. This means that the speakers and trainers must be comfortable addressing separate but similar audiences on common issues. It's mandatory to finish off the agenda with one or more common events. Group workshops and panel discussions help spread new ideas and insights across both groups. As well, I like to have a closing banquet with the seating arranged so that the two groups are mixed for the maximum amount of cross-pollination.

Satellite Agenda

Another agenda format, the satellite agenda, is used for conventions and association meetings. It's made up of a series of separate seminars that revolve around and integrate with a focal master event such as a trade show or plenary session. To work well, this agenda requires a great deal of preparation and preregistration. Otherwise, you can wind up with standing room only at one session while several others are empty. A sample agenda is as follows.

1. Workshops A, B, C, D in Rooms 1, 2, 3, 4
2. Workshops E, F, G in Rooms 5, 6, 7
3. Presentations H, I, J, K in Rooms 8, 9, 10, 11
4. Plenary session/suppliers' exhibits in Room 12
5. Breakout sessions L, M, N in Rooms 1, 2, 3
6. Breakout sessions O, P, Q, R in Rooms 4, 5, 6, 7
7. Closing banquet and guest speaker

This sort of meeting requires the right kind of venue, with a good supply of breakout rooms. Convention centers can handle a satellite agenda as can some large hotels. I have also seen it work well on a university campus, with classrooms used for seminars and a large auditorium as the plenary area. If you use a summer resort, some sessions can be run outdoors.

Choosing Your Agenda

You might base your meeting on one of these agenda types or you might decide on a variation of one of them or a combination of more than one. Your choice will be based on the strategic directives that have guided your thinking to this point. You shouldn't have any trouble choosing the right agenda format if you follow these steps:

1. Review the original objectives in detail, discussing them with other senior executives.

2. Review the strategy derived from those objectives and the research.

3. Meetings are held for purposes of information transmission, problem solving, learning, and motivation. Which of these do you want to address and in what priority?

4. Select an agenda layout or variation that gives you the mechanism most clearly suited to your objectives.

I once went through this process with a client whose business is selling airtime on television and radio to advertising agencies. The objective of the conference was to improve company morale, as measured by interviews before and after the event. We decided on a strategy of giving the attendees plenty of opportunity to discuss common issues on an informal basis. We identified information, learning, and motivation as the major needs. Information was important because pre-meeting interviews had identified a high need to know about specific issues. We also identified a demand for new sales training, specifically negotiating skills. Finally, motivation was a key issue because head office neglect and apathy had engendered a lot of negative emotions.

We settled on a sandwich agenda because it would allow us to transmit information easily while giving the attendees plenty of time to think about it and absorb it. It is also the best agenda for networking, which tends to be a boon to motivation because it gives people a chance to compare notes and identify problems in a relaxed atmosphere. The other standard agenda formats were too rigidly structured for what we wanted to achieve at this meeting. The final agenda was as follows.

First day

First block: 6:00 p.m.   Opening dinner
                  7:30   Audio-visual: *Our Yesterday: Fifty Years of Success*
                  7:40   Keynote address by company president: "Today's Issues Affecting Our Company"
                  8:30   Presentation of conference objectives
                  9:00   Assignments for the next day

End of first session

Second day

Main body: 7:00 a.m.   Breakfast
                  8:00   Opening workshops
                  10:00   Refreshment break
                  10:30   Plenary session to review field office information
                  11:15   Training session: "Identifying Unique Client Needs"
                  12:00 p.m.   Lunch
                  1:30   Panel discussion: "Where Business May Be Going"
                  3:00   Refreshment break and free time

End of main body

Third block:
                  5:30 p.m.   Training workshop: "Selling Through Emotions"
                  6:30   Review of conference assignments
                  7:00   General discussion of action plans
                  7:45   Review of objectives and evaluation
                  8:00   Closing dinner

The chart in Figure 4–1 can help you to choose which kind of agenda is best suited to your meeting.

Figure 4-1 Choosing the Best Agenda

	Mirror-Image	Sandwich	Parallel	Satellite
Information	excellent	excellent	good	excellent
Problem solving	excellent	good	excellent	excellent
Learning	excellent	excellent	very good	excellent
Motivation	fair	excellent	good	fair

As you can see, no one agenda covers every contingency. Therefore, a variation or combination might best suit your requirements. If, for example, you were to combine a parallel set of sandwich agendas, you would be able, at least in principle, to cover every situation. There's a risk, however, of an agenda becoming too complex, crowded, and exhausting. Attendees will rebel against agendas that try to do too much in too little time. It's best, therefore, not to get overambitious. In large meetings, less is usually more.

5

BRINGING DISCIPLINE TO YOUR PLAN

Until now, you and your team have been concentrating on the task of designing a strategy and plan for a meeting that will achieve a specific result. There comes a time, however, to begin coordinating the logistics.

A meeting is a series of events — audio-visuals, guest speakers, workshops, entertainment, relaxation. The art of program management is the art of making certain that these events happen according to your overall plan. These events must be contained within a definite schedule and a definite budget. You'll need at least three teams — one to work on the hotel accommodations, one on the technical side (such things as audio-visuals and staging), and a third on the program. All of these elements are then integrated into an overall strategic design.

Since strategy dictates the plan and the plan dictates logistics, all logistical decisions must be related to the message you want to convey. Suppose your message is that in your organization, individuals are important. If a hotel is chosen that treats your attendees as a crowd rather than as individuals, your purpose will be defeated. The experience that people have in a meeting has a direct relationship to the message they will take home with them.

Coaching the Teams

Teams need clearly stated objectives. They should understand the overall objective of the meeting as well as the purpose of the aspect on which they are working. They must be willing to

71

accept responsibility for making sure their objectives are met. It's up to the travel and accommodations team, for example, to make sure that everyone arrives safely and gets satisfactory accommodation.

Teams need resources, both money and time. In determining how much money and time are needed, a good rule of thumb is to make your best estimate and add ten percent. There is no point in having objectives and then refusing to allot the resources needed to meet them. If your plan is to put 250 people into high-quality rooms, the budget must be realistic. It can't be done for $50 per person. Obtain information from the experts — hotels, airlines, audio-visual specialists — before setting your budget.

Meeting coordination often goes awry because not enough time is allocated to do the job. Someone says, "Find us a hotel; you've got six weeks." The unfortunate fact is that in some areas it's hard to book a large group into a good hotel even six months in advance. Most meetings are held in the fall or in the spring. Hotel space for those periods should be booked *at least* three months in advance. Advance planning is also needed for travel and other arrangements. Producing an audio-visual is neither a two-day nor a two-week process. It often takes two months or more.

Drawing Up the Schedule

Scheduling is diagramming. You'll find examples in this chapter of flowchart schedules that are designed to help an individual or a team manage a program over a period of time. A flowchart is a graphic depiction of what has to be done by whom and when.

The flowchart schedule involves deciding how much time you will need to complete each project. Although a flowchart schedule can appear very complex, it should be relatively easy to follow. Figure 5–1 illustrates only a portion of a meeting plan flowchart schedule. This type of attention to detail and the time it takes will be well worth the effort.

A flowchart schedule is an excellent monitoring tool, allowing you to see at a glance what is happening and when. A schedule also instills discipline into the meeting planning process. It is your best weapon against the natural inclination of many people to stall and dither until a deadline is fast approaching and then rush like mad to get the project done. That natural inclination

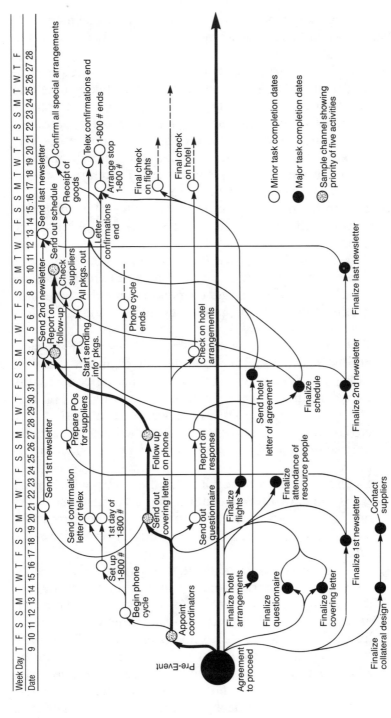

Figure 5–1 A partial pre-event schedule flowchart

leads to sloppy, late work. The following outlines the manner in which a flowchart schedule for your meeting is created.

1. Establish a start date for the whole process. Let's assume you're planning a meeting of three hundred people outside the country. Today is January 2 and your first decision has to be made on January 25. That's your start date.

2. Establish a delivery date for the entire project. A very important person in your organization wants the meeting in June because golfing is best then. Therefore, you pick June 25 as the final day of your meeting.

3. Determine the total number of units (days) from start to finish of the project. In this case, it's 152 because you count holidays and weekends.

4. List, in order of priority, the major tasks that need to be done to produce the meeting — choosing a theme, designing a logo, creating an agenda, picking a hotel or other site, finding a travel agent, producing audio-visuals, developing a registration program, and so on.

5. Place the major task completion dates at appropriate points in the 152-day schedule. For example, if airline tickets must be booked thirty days in advance to qualify for a discount, place the completion of this task on Day 122. If that day is a holiday or weekend, move it to the closest working day earlier in the schedule. These tasks are usually placed below the center line as shown in Figure 5–1.

6. Determine which major tasks connect with which other tasks and draw lines to connect them. For instance, if the hotel confirmation ties in with the airline confirmation, as it often does, connect these two directly even if they are on different days.

7. Take each major task and break it down into smaller tasks. Determine delegation and decision points — times for delegating work and making decisions yourself. For example, organizing your registration program requires lining up assistance and printing registration materials. You delegate the search for registration helpers and the actual printing of the materials. Decision tasks, however, are choosing the best individuals to handle the registration and approving a design for the registration materials.

8. Establish a time priority for each minor task and place it at a point before the major task completion. Suppose you've chosen Day 30 for completion of a task. You've got five minor tasks, from Priority 1 to Priority 5. You make sure that both the start and completion dates of Priority 1 are situated first in your schedule. The least important item will be completed last and the most important will be completed first. (See Figure 5–1.)

9. Now comes the actual scheduling system. For each minor task, establish a minimum and maximum amount of time that you think you'll need. There are two ways to do this. One is by talking to people who have done similar tasks. The second is by consulting experts in the relevant area.

   Suppose the task is having an audio-visual script written. You've never done this before. First, you have to establish the theme of the script, the issues it's going to deal with, and the information it's going to convey. This must be done long before you get it written up professionally. To determine how long it's going to take to get the script done, call someone in the audio-visual business to get a time estimate.

10. Once you've got the time estimate, add it to your estimates for your other tasks — choosing the theme, issues, and information. Come up with a best-case and a worst-case time. If the best is twenty days and the worst is sixty days, the average is forty days — and that's what goes on your schedule. If you've determined that the script has to be completed on Day 92, then you work back forty days to find that your start date is Day 52.

11. Now you make the internal connections between the major and minor tasks. Visualize the connections between all the major steps in the meeting — program, accommodations, transportation — as the trunk of a tree. From that trunk grow many branches, which themselves have numerous offshoots. An example is sending out letters of confirmation to all attendees flying in on a certain day. This would be an offshoot of the preregistration branch. Sending out letters of confirmation also might interconnect with your teaser campaign. But don't connect those two directly on your flowchart or you'll wind

up with a diagram that looks like a railway switching yard. Instead, connect everything back through the trunk.

12. You now have a flowchart that begins at a realistic start date and proceeds to a completion date, passing through each important and interrelated step, based on actual fact and informed estimates.

Throughout your schedule, it's important that you distinguish between delegation and decision. You must isolate those points at which you have to make decisions. As the meeting planner, only you can decide whether to book the Hilton or the Holiday Inn. On the other hand, decisions about sending out mailings can be delegated.

A flowchart schedule usually runs for several months although I've done several that went as long as a year and a half, from Day 1 of planning to the end of an extended follow-up period. A "clock" ticks off along the top of your schedule, marking the decision-making and delegation points. If a decision is made for a certain hotel, you should be able to relate that to the next item. It may be that you have to delegate somebody to go and work out a letter of agreement with the hotel. The schedule triggers a series of consequences for every decision-making point. Note in the diagram how every decision-making and delegation point is connected to other decision-making points all along the time line.

Since you work backward from the completion date in setting up the schedule, everything you do is directly tied to end results. Every consequence is the tip of an iceberg of steps and logical events. The lines of connection travel effortlessly back to a whole line of events at some earlier starting point. True, a few events are discrete occurrences — they don't depend on anything else. But the vast majority of your tasks as you prepare the meeting consists of a whole series of precursor tasks, decisions, and information, all of which can be connected and identified. The flowchart schedule is a representation of reality as a process.

Murphy's Law Antidote

You've set up teams staffed with able people. The teams have clear divisions of responsibility. And now you've got a detailed schedule that tells you what will happen, where and when it will

Figure 5-2 Murphy's Law Antidote

Checklist # __2__   Registration   Date: <u>August/88</u>

#	Step or Item	Date	Problem	Prevention	Remedy
1	Attendance finalized	20	Hold outs	Stress urgency of reply	Telex requesting immediate RSVP
2	Notify everyone of above	22	Hold outs	Warn of possibility	Send out list to date
3	Appoint Registrar Team	22	Not enough	Request volunteers (give time off)	Ask hotel for personnel
4	Familiarize team	29	No time	Request after-hours session	Take a weekend to do
5	Lost and found area arranged	10	Not available	Mention early to hotel	Request extra hotel room
6	Check insurance company	10	No insurance	Discuss with hotel	Take out 3-day policy
7	Type up name tags	10	Not enough	Discuss with hotel	Use buttons and tape
8	Type emerg. info' on name tags	10	Not enough	See item #7	See item #7
9	Photocopy materials	10	Not enough	Request hotel machine	Use hotel machine
10	Obtain TTC ride guide	10	Unavailable	Ask hotel to get it for you	Call Board of Trade
11	Obtain TTC tokens	10	Not enough	Ask staging company to provide	Get from subway station
12	Print peel-and-stick labels	12	Not enough	Keep extras in supply	Discuss with hotel
13	Run role-play session	15	No time	See item #4	See item #4
14	Arrange for coffee	16	None foreseen	None	None
15	Set up coffee	17	Unavailable	Set explicit times with hotel	Get some soft drinks outside
16	All registrars present	17	Missing	Have 2 spares	Ask hotel to provide
17	Set up registrar's table	17	Unavailable	Have extra in room	Rent from staging company
18	Table cover & skirt	17	Unavailable	See item #17	See item #17
19	Chairs, etc.	17	Unavailable	Have extras in room	Get from hotel rooms
20	Name tags, buttons	17	Not enough	Make sure you have	Print up on foamboard
21	Printed/copied materials	17	Not enough	See item #9	See item #9
22	Posters & cards	17	Unavailable	Take pencil linears to meeting	Hand-draw on foamboard
23	Register & pens	17	Unavailable	Discuss with hotel	Use foolscap instead
24					
25					
26					
27					
28					
29					
30					

happen, and who will do what. That's fine but it doesn't guarantee that everything will go smoothly. There always are problems and obstacles, things that don't go quite the way they should or according to schedule. To cope with the inevitable, you need a review procedure.

First of all, you need checklists. In creating your flowchart diagram you have already listed major and minor tasks in order of priority. You therefore have most of what you need for a good checklist. However, the checklist goes into greater detail, covering even subtasks that are assumed but not written down in the flowchart schedule. With your checklist, you can follow what should be happening day by day and verify that indeed it is happening. A simpler type of checklist just lists everything that should be done point by point.

Figure 5-2 represents what I call "Murphy's Law Antidote." Murphy's Law states that if anything can go wrong, it will. The antidote is to identify potential problems in advance, along with ways to prevent them or, if that is impossible, to remedy them when they occur. For example, if you are going to need a decision from a senior executive, assume that he or she will fail to make that decision. The preventive measure might be to identify another senior executive who would be able to make the same decision. If that doesn't work, the remedial action might be to assign a secretary with good access to the executive to pester him or her into making the decision.

All of this takes considerable foresight on the part of your planning team but the effort will be rewarded — anticipating problems is the best way to avoid them. When the the meeting is over, you can consult your Murphy's Law Antidote and note which problems occurred that weren't listed. That way you'll be a smarter meeting planner the next time around. You'll never be perfect, but you can keep getting better.

6

PUTTING MAGIC INTO YOUR MEETING

Suppose your organization is going through some tough times. Perhaps it has had to reorganize, dropping entire production units and eliminating jobs. You have decided to call the remaining employees together in a meeting to reassure them about the future. How should that meeting be handled? Although this is a time when hard realities must be faced, perhaps the best strategy might be to use play-acting.

There are theater groups that specialize in performing for large meetings. It's on occasions like this that their services are particularly useful. What you have to do at this meeting is relieve the surviving employees' uncertainty by showing them a positive vision of the future. It's difficult to do this if you are restricted to the regular, two-dimensional tools of meeting communications such as speakers, workshops, and seminars.

Live theater can make the future come alive. The magic of theater lies in the "suspension of disbelief." Dim the lights and open the curtain on a stage, and an audience is willing to believe that it's witnessing another time and another place. Amazingly, your audience may be much more willing to accept a message from the mouths of actors in a darkened theater than that same message told in a matter-of-fact way by you in a brightly lit meeting room.

For best effect, the play should be followed by a special kind of speaker, a motivational speaker who can step down from the podium, walk among the audience, and involve people both emotionally and intellectually in your organization's new future. Finding such a speaker, who would have to have some background in your field, may take some digging but it's worth the extra effort because it takes a special kind of person to make your people understand the need for change and for preparing themselves for the challenges ahead.

Industrial theater and special speakers are two categories of what I call "special elements." Others are special packages of learning materials and special effects. You couldn't afford to use these special elements at every meeting. And you don't *need* them at every meeting because they're often neither necessary nor appropriate.

Suppose this same downsized company holds its annual sales conference a few weeks later. The purpose of that meeting is to dispense information about company sales and to hone the selling skills of the sales force. The standard meeting tools — marketing presentations, audio-visuals, seminars, information kits, and workshops — will do the job. These people have now been reassured about the future. And as salespeople, they are most comfortable with practical, immediately usable material. There's no need to put on a special show.

Choosing the Right Resource Person

GUEST SPEAKER

There are four kinds of resource people for this special type of meeting — guest speakers, consultants, trainers, and moderators. You're probably wondering why I'm defining a guest speaker as a special element. After all, every meeting has guest speakers. What's special about that? Well, there are speakers and there are speakers. I'm not talking here about some local politician or other dignitary dropping in to say a few words or organization officials with their annual remarks. I am talking about individuals with unique talents and knowledge brought in to deal in a highly specific manner with the problem the meeting has been called to address.

Such a speaker is often the focal point of a meeting. He or she addresses the issue as an objective, outside observer whose name and independent status give him or her a credibility that no organization official can claim. This type of speaker has a particular point of view and special expertise that is going to be used to help introduce a major change such as a reorganization, address a major issue such as deregulation, or help solve a major problem.

A key characteristic of this special speaker is that he or she interacts with the audience in a special way, stimulating the audience in a way that guarantees feedback. Ken Blanchard, author of *The One-Minute Manager*, speaking to a group of managers in a company trying to change its management style, is a special element. Karl Albrecht, co-author of *Servicing America*, also played such a role when a major bank invited him to help improve its customer service. Albrecht is a consultant with impressive experience in upgrading customer service. He was able to bring theory to life in setting the stage for a series of how-to workshops that the bank was holding in a major effort to reorient its corporate culture toward service.

A multinational building supplies conglomerate wanted to change from being a production-oriented to a market-oriented company. It wanted the research and development process within each of its twelve divisions to be more sensitive to customer demand. The motivation for this desire to change was that the company was losing market share to competitors who were coming out with more successful new products than it was.

To help, the company brought in Robert Keidel, a professor at the Wharton School of Business at the University of Pennsylvania. His specialty is demonstrating the similarities between the organization of sports teams and that of companies. Some companies are organized like football teams, with the coach sending in orders from the sidelines on every play. In other games, such as hockey and basketball, the players constantly have to make their own split-second decisions.

Keidel analyzed each of the twelve divisions to discover what "game" it should be playing. For example, he decided that some divisions should be playing basketball because they had to adjust to rapid changes in market conditions and required a tightly knit defense against competitive advances. Others needed to take as their game a special hybrid of football, baseball, or hockey. Being sports-minded, the managers responded well to this analysis and worked with Keidel to change the rules of the game in their divisions in order to score more marketing points.

Finding the right speaker takes some research on the part of the meeting planner. The speaker should be someone with a background in your field. Someone might have a good reputation as a motivational speaker but can't be asked to deal with a key issue if he or she has no background in it. The meeting planner should canvass people within your field for suggestions or hire a meetings specialist to do the search.

A high-quality speaker will cost approximately $3,000, although the fee can run as high as $25,000 for a big name such as Tom Peters. Expenses, including hotel and air fare, are extra.

Don't allow anyone on your team to be intimidated by guest speakers, no matter how eminent and successful they may be, who refuse to ally themselves with your strategy. Your guest speaker is being paid well and if that speaker is worth the price, he or she won't just parachute in, give two cents' worth of service, and take off.

I've had speakers like that but I've never invited them back a second time. I've told them bluntly that, although their fee would be paid, it wasn't earned because they talked about everything except what I wanted them to talk about.

You can't tell your speaker what to say and how to say it. But you've chosen that speaker because his or her area of expertise is relevant to the theme of your meeting. Write down a list of the key points you would like the speaker to stress. An experienced, professional speaker will be happy to cooperate.

CONSULTANT

The second category of resource person is the consultant. He or she is brought in to do one specific task. For example, I have used Roy Jones, an internationally known specialist in creative problem solving, also known as brainstorming. When there is a major problem to be solved, he finds new and unusual ways to arrive at solutions.

The most successful industrialists of our time are the Japanese. But even they have something to learn from Roy who has instructed leading Japanese scientists, engineers, and businessmen on the use of brainstorming techniques to build creativity.

You wouldn't bring in a Roy Jones to a rest-and-relaxation meeting or a gathering meant to celebrate a major organization success. Those aren't occasions for brainstorming. His talent is a special one and it is appropriate only on special occasions.

TRAINER

The third category is a trainer or a training company. A trainer is a consultant who specializes in designing learning tools and curriculums. Learning Dynamics, of Calgary, and Laura Miller and Associates, which has offices in several North American cities, are two of many training companies whose services are on the market.

A trainer will devise a training course for a specific purpose for a specific meeting. In one meeting, we were launching a new food product, specially packaged fruit juices. We used a trainer to help the salespeople to understand the emotional appeal that the product had for grocery store buyers.

The trainer analyzed the various features of the product and then challenged each salesperson to put himself or herself into the shoes of the customer, taking the features of these neat little packages and showing the buyer how those features were to his or her benefit. The trainer understood, in a way that the marketing manager of the company did not, the techniques of this kind of analysis and how to explain it.

MODERATOR

The fourth resource person is the moderator, also known as a facilitator or master of ceremonies. These people are the glue that pulls everything together. They are skilled at getting individuals to work together as a group. They have a knack for establishing rapport quickly with an audience. They are skilled interpreters, they know how to sum up, consolidate, and clarify half a dozen different ideas that are being discussed at the same time. These people are buyers and sellers of ideas who never lose sight of the goal the meeting is trying to achieve. They are consensus builders and problem solvers and are often excellent speakers.

You only call on the services of a moderator when you need a catalyst who can be seen as an objective friend and leader who is "untainted" by being in the employ of your organization. He or she is both "above the meeting" in the sense of being an outsider and "inside the meeting" in that he or she is sympathetic, understanding, and knowledgeable about what's going on.

If you are dealing with a touchy subject or introducing new concepts you may need a moderator. Running an open session on a controversial issue such as, for example, sexual harrassment in the workplace, isn't simple. It requires a moderator who can stand above the meeting and impose order on it, yet at the same time encourage people to take part.

How do you find the moderator you need? As with guest speakers, often the best ones are former executives with experience in your field or a related one, who may have set up shop as consultants. Experience in your organization's field is important because one of the challenges for a moderator, for example, in an open session, is identifying issues when they come up. Of equal importance is the distance and objectivity that they, as outsiders, can bring to your meeting. That is why in-house trainers and MCs often don't work out. You must weigh the objectivity value of an outsider with the knowledge that an insider has, and determine which is most needed at your meeting.

The Props

Each meeting requires new and different props or packages. Packages are self-contained collections of learning materials designed to fit into a meeting for a specific use. They aren't transferrable from one situation to another without extensive modification. As special elements, they aren't designed for everyday use. There are several kinds of packages, including audio-visuals, training modules, workbooks, and computer programs.

AUDIO-VISUALS

Audio-visuals include films, tapes, slides, overheads, and sound tapes. A generic audio-visual is one with a standard theme — for instance, "Do Your Best" — that can be customized for a specific meeting. The people attending the meeting, or the head office, or services, machinery, or products of the organization holding the meeting, are worked into the audio-visual.

We have often used a generic audio-visual that gives a coast-to-coast tour of the country, mixing stirring music and magnificent scenery with glimpses of the organization and its people in action. This approach is successful because it associates pride in one's nation with pride in the organization and makes the organization part of a larger entity.

An advantage of using generic audio-visuals is that they cost about forty percent less than having one made to order, or roughly $4,000 instead of $10,000. Furthermore, if an item has been successful in the past, chances are it will be successful again in the future. One of the best is "Reach for the Top," an inspiring piece about the scaling of Mount Everest. You can customize it for your organization but only for a specific situation such as sales motivation, the idea being that salespeople too can reach a peak.

Film or video offers you tremendous power of movement, color, and sound. You use it when you want a larger-than-life, theatrical effect. Video is fast replacing film. It can be altered more easily and technological improvements have given it almost the clarity and crispness of film.

A recent development is interactive videodiscs. This technology allows quick access to any point on a videodisc. The audience can be led up to a decision point or a simulated real-life situation and then asked to choose from several options.

These are very expensive, costing anywhere from $40,000 to $250,000. The high cost might be justified, for example, in the case of a large chain of retail shoe stores that wanted to use it to train sales personnel. The narrator would say, "Here comes the customer, she's going to ask you a question and you have to answer it."

The trainee types in his or her answer and then the narrator on the videodisc responds, "That was fine but I suggest you say this instead. Would you like to try it over again?" A huge selection of different responses can be stored on the disc. This technology is most useful in cases where people can't easily get to the training location; the training program goes to them. The technology is still in its infancy but it's developing quickly and eventually will become less expensive.

You can do the same thing, but with a much more limited range of responses, using videotape, which is much cheaper than videodiscs. In a launch of a cleaning product, I ran a tape showing a supermarket buyer, the person who would make the decision on whether his store would stock the product. One member of the audience would make a sales presentation and the buyer, played by an actor, responded, "What's so special about this cleanser? It's just the same old stuff."

The audience had to choose from among three responses: 1) It's been totally changed. 2) It represents more value for the money. 3) It has a better scouring capability than the old one.

The buyer's reaction to all three responses were on the videotape. Once the audience chose a response, the tape played his reaction to that response. At the end of the exercise, everyone discussed what had happened. It would have been cheaper to have a real buyer on hand to work through this exercise but that wouldn't have given the same larger-than-life impact that we achieved using a professional script and professional actor.

Production of interactive videotapes requires a lot of expensive projection equipment. The cost of staging them represents about thirty to forty percent of the actual production cost, so that an interactive videotape costing $15,000 requires an additional $5,000 to $7,000 in rental costs for technical staff and equipment.

TRAINING MODULES

Another type of package is the training module. These are packaged training presentations on video tape. A trainer is present and he or she will supervise a group of about fifteen trainees in a half-day session. The combination of live instruction from the trainer plus exercises and role playing involving the video can result in a strong educational impact in a short period of time.

Perhaps you want to teach people how to analyze your services or products for emotional appeals that will bring positive results. A training module could be customized to address the unique features of your organization. A few companies specialize in taking actual case histories and anecdotes relating to an organization and customizing a training module around them.

A training module should focus on one new skill to be learned, because it's impossible in one meeting to do more than one or two things well. Two skills well learned are like a surface to which you can attach a lot of other training. But try to teach a dozen things and you'll succeed in teaching none. Worse, you'll leave your people with no basis on which to acquire new learning.

WORKBOOKS

Most people who attend business meetings have seen some sort of workbook. Too often they comprise just a pile of material hurriedly slapped together and stuffed into a binder. What a workbook should be is a carefully designed series of exercises. It might involve cassettes, graphics, flowcharts, and case histories. It is intended to be used after the meeting as well as during it, because it's a reinforcement of the message of the meeting.

I organized a meeting for two hundred members of an association of moving companies during a time when the moving industry was in turmoil because of government deregulation. No one knew how deregulation would affect them and no one knew what they should do about it.

The purpose of the meeting was to identify threats to the industry posed by this new situation and to develop responses. The workbook played a crucial role because it contained all the key data. It included a description of the problem, case histories and real-life scenarios, background information, and a brainstorming form.

The workbook also summarized the key points in a skit, *Monday at the Movers*, that had opened the meeting. The skit illustrated some of the probable results of deregulation — more competition, more demanding customers, a shortage of good employees.

A specialist in developing ideas worked with the attendees on ways to create effective solutions through the use of lateral thinking, a concept developed by Edward de Bono, a British psychologist. The attendees broke up into groups of twenty people, each led by a facilitator whose purpose was to brainstorm ideas. The ideas were put down on the brainstorming forms, which were laid out as follows:

- tasks to be done
- persons responsible for those tasks
- time frames for completion of the tasks
- flowcharts establishing priorities of tasks and interrelationships among them
- references, including books and articles

The workbook was the master organizer to the follow-up that was undertaken by the association's management. Any materials sent out later were designed to fit into the book.

Workbooks are most appropriate to any meeting that requires fast results. That excludes most meetings having a recreational or motivational purpose; neither of those messages fit into the workbook format. But if you are problem solving or developing action plans or learning new skills, you probably could use a workbook to advantage.

Meeting or training consultants are experienced in coordinating the job of putting the workbook together. If you do not wish to use outside expertise, your human resource manager may be the best person to take charge of the job. He or she will have to assume the role of editor and work with all the contributors to the meeting to create a workbook that includes a balance of information, training materials, and testing devices.

COMPUTER PROGRAMS

One of the most popular types of package currently is computer programs. Computer terminals are useful for imparting information that can be learned through a question-and-answer format.

Computers can be linked to videodisc players to provide a program in which a person is shown a skill, tries the skill, and has it analyzed by the computer.

An example is a medical program on cardiopulmonary resuscitation (CPR) that is available through most heart associations. The trainee watches a video on CPR techniques and then is instructed to try each step on a dummy that is attached to a computer. The dummy monitors such things as the pressure the trainee puts on the chest, the force of air blown into the lungs, and the timing. If anything is done wrongly, the computer turns the videodisc on to the relevant point and repeats the instruction.

Because they cost many thousands of dollars, these high-technology items we've discussed aren't for everyone. I'm not suggesting that they should be acquired for one meeting only. They are meant to be used on a regular basis, as reinforcements for trainer-led courses already in place.

The key factor in deciding whether such an investment is justified is volume of use, which isn't necessarily the same as number of users. If you have fifty people using the package ten times, your volume of use is the same as that of some company with five hundred people using it once. If spending $200,000 will net several million in increased sales, the expenditure is probably justified. But never forget that technology itself is no panacea.

Industrial Theater

Industrial theater is the transmitting of information through entertainment. Like any other kind of theater it requires a script, actors, a stage, lighting, sound, a director, and a crew.

Every population center larger than a hamlet has actors, comedians, singers, belly dancers, and other entertainers for hire. Your meeting planners can check the telephone book yellow pages under "Convention Services" and "Entertainment Bureaus" for the necessary information for putting the production together.

Industrial theater is particularly valuable when you are dealing with delicate issues such as the reorganization I discussed at the beginning of this chapter. If your team is considering the use of theater, make sure that they give themselves lots of time. From the script conference that begins the process to actual staging of the production, two to three months might be necessary, at cost of at least $20,000.

I used theater in a large meeting for a telecommunications company that was undergoing what it euphemistically called "internal uncertainties." In five years, the place had been reorganized three times. We wanted to get the message across that everything was now settled down and the future would be one of positive change.

It was a touchy situation because these uncertainties had been badly handled in the past and, if badly handled again, could only increase the employees' skepticism. The salespeople were young, well educated, and aggressive. They were people who moved at a brisk pace and were almost incapable of sitting still.

The actors had to acquire this way of moving in order to play these people believably. They succeeded. Also, the professional scriptwriter had dealt with a number of delicate issues in an entertaining fashion, making an emotion-charged issue more palatable.

On another occasion, the audience itself was involved in the play. At a convention dealing with the effects of new competition into a crowded packaged-goods market, we ran a skit on the theme of marketing "warfare." People were picked up by buses painted in camouflage colors and staffed with actors dressed as commandos. They were taken to a sports camp and given watered-down boot camp training by actors pretending to be army officers.

Everyone got fatigue-type T-shirts. They took target practice with air rifles and attacked an easy obstacle course. Of course, there were also lessons on how to make "war" on the competition, which was the point of it all. The attendees immediately began to identify similarities between military combat and corporate combat. They understood how discipline and mental toughness could keep a diverse bunch of individuals working as a team. They learned how concentrated attention on a well-defined objective can lead to capturing that objective. Finally, they learned how to begin a defensive maneuver and then switch into the offensive.

Special Effects

The audience was seated in the dark, looking at a blank screen.

The only sound was the peaceful rippling of a quiet lake. Then, in the distance, came the noise of an approaching motor boat. Then the din of motor boats started to fill the room from all sides.

Images appeared on the screen of water being churned by the speeding boats. Curtains next to the stage parted and revealed actual motor boats. Then, the camera went inside an outboard motor, and the accompanying sound effects simulated what one would hear if one were actually inside: sparks crackling, pistons moving, and an overhead explosion.

All of this was by way of introduction to a meeting for an outboard motor company that was bringing out a new, quieter outboard motor for fishermen who don't want noisy boats that scare away the fish.

Special effects add magic to your meeting. People sense that something wonderful is happening that's out of their control. Special effects can be awe-inspiring; they help to bring about an open-mindedness among attendees at a meeting. When people are in that frame of mind, they are ready to be motivated.

I did a meeting for an international accounting firm, which ended with an announcement of a major change in the organization, involving the use of computer systems. To dramatize the change, we arranged an indoor, computer-generated fireworks display inside the meeting room. You can do fabulous things with all sorts of lights — spotlights, moving lights, lasers, and mirror balls, which are those large, mirrored balls that decorate dance halls and give a starlight effect when a spotlight shines on them. You can combine light and sound to create a spectacular show.

It was an important change for the accounting firm and the aim of the spectacle was to make the attendees feel positive about it. So we went all out. We had a stationary screen from the ceiling to the front of the stage. It was made of Tyvec, a synthetic fabric that is highly reflective. Fifty-six slide projectors were connected to an audio-visual synchronizing computer that generated the "fireworks." The accompanying stereotape supplied the pops, bangs, whistles, and booms of the noisiest fireworks display.

Moving screens are yet another special effect. You might have a multi-image show, with parts of the screen moving on and off the stage or backward and forward. One of the most effective uses of moving screens can be seen at Disney World. It's a method for illustrating the relative importance of different pieces of information.

For example, you might have three separate screens in place on the stage. On cue, one of them moves forward. You could use this technique to great effect if you were trying to point out, for example, that the only solution to an internal misunderstanding is to open up and talk about it. You might have one of the screens move forward with a close-up of a senior officer saying, "Let's talk." It's dramatic and can have a big impact on the audience.

An old standby among special effects is the marquee, a big outdoor tent that lends a carnival atmsophere to a meeting. It can be used outdoors or indoors if you have a large meeting space, as in a convention center. You might consider renting a marquee if you want to highlight something at a meeting, such as some new program or state-of-the-art equipment.

A special effect with strong dramatic impact is the presentation of an audio-visual on a large outdoor screen on a warm summer evening. I ran a meeting for a high-tech producer of electrical contacts for the computer industry. This company wanted to bring home the point to its salespeople that it was the vanguard of the industry. We ran a video and slide show under the stars showing a spaceship landing on Earth. An alien walked out and said, "We're here to destroy the earth because you are not technologically advanced enough." Then the president of the company engaged him in an argument about technological advancement and demonstrated the advantages of his company's product. He talked the alien out of destroying the earth. It was all tongue-in-cheek, of course, but the presentation was dramatic, it was a lovely summer night, and the audience loved it.

An outdoor screen can be set up in your organization's parking lot or grounds or you could actually rent a drive-in theater. Or you could set the screen up on the shore of a lake and have your audience watch from boats. A picnic might be the ideal setting for showing an audio-visual this way.

Yet another special effect is a magic act, which is an enjoyable way to introduce a new product. You could use a professional magician as moderator of the meeting, having him or her spring magic on the audience at intervals. In a product launch, for example, the magician could make the new product appear out of nowhere. Or he or she could demonstrate the product's magic by making printed statements attesting to its features, strengths, and sales appeal materialize from thin air.

Dry ice and real fireworks displays also can be used to create excitement, but some of these special effects should be handled only by professionals. A professional meeting planner can advise on when and how to utilize special effects and which ones fit best with your meeting's goal, your strategy for achieving that goal, and the budget with which you have to work. Put your imagination to work. If you can dream it, you can do it.

7

FOLLOW-UP FOR FUTURE PLANNING

In designing a plan for any event, you and your team must consider the two hundred or so days of the year during which the members of your audience are working at their regular jobs. Follow-up is the process of actively pursuing the results of a meeting into those two hundred days. Certain attitudes or practices or new policies will be identified during the meeting as promising long-term benefits to the organization and its members. Follow-up tries to turn that promise into a reality. You must always prepare for follow-up *before* the actual event takes place; otherwise you lose the impact of careful targeting.

Follow-up uses everything positive about the meeting while trying to come to an honest understanding and resolution of the negatives. Suppose a company's operations managers go on a retreat to examine ways to improve productivity. They come up with twelve good ideas, of which none can easily be implemented. Eight are very expensive and the others would require a fundamental rethinking of the entire operational procedure.

Follow-up must pursue the positive purpose of that meeting by keeping alive the enthusiasm and belief the attendees had in the ideas they generated. It should continue the spirit of the retreat by occasionally bringing the group together again, even if only through a conference call. Follow-up should ensure that each person knows what he or she must do to marshal the resources to see those changes through. This may require an action plan outlining a set of tasks, assigning responsibilities for them, and deadlines for their completion.

Follow-up is a way of making sure that the investment you

made in a meeting pays dividends. That is why it is the planning team's responsibility. Follow-up builds on the foundation that was laid down by the meeting. It can allow you to realize those dividends whether the reaction to your meeting was good or bad.

Surprisingly, a negative reaction can lead to positive dividends. Suppose you invested a lot of money in a lavish meeting only to hear that it was a load of hype lacking in substance. That reaction may be telling you that your organization needs to be more open with its people than it has in the past. If the organization acts on that insight, the ultimate results of the poorly received meeting may be healthy.

Follow-up is a way of bridging between meetings. The business year consists of approximately 217 working days. Often it seems to lack all sense of a beginning, middle, or end. There's no feeling of development, direction, or evolution. Follow-up imparts some definition to your year because you can't carry out a follow-up program without planning and schedules and deadlines.

Because it requires participation from many people, follow-up aids in the development of an organization. One executive or one planning team member can't follow up by himself or herself.

Most organizations pay lip service to the importance of planning for the future. "Oh yes," they'll say, "we have long-range plans. We're a modern organization, looking forward to the twenty-first century." But far from looking ahead to the next century, they won't even look ahead to the next meeting. If you close your doors on your meeting when it wraps up and don't give it another thought, you're saying, in effect, that you're in business for today only and forget about tomorrow.

Doing follow-up forces you to adopt a long-range attitude in your thinking. You can't do it in an ad hoc way because follow-up and ad hoc decision making mix like oil and water. You'll either become a strategic thinker or you'll stop doing follow-up. Practicing follow-up gives a clear signal that your organization means business, that it takes things seriously, that it's in the game for keeps.

Building Bridges

I've often been told by executives that once they've done a fantastic meeting, their biggest problem is that they have to worry about doing a better one next year. I always ask them, "What do you do about it between meetings? If you've had a good meeting, that means good things happened that should have been pursued. How did you pursue them?"

If you didn't pursue them, getting ready for the next meeting is going to be a major task. If you did, those good things will develop and give you all the direction you need. In most cases, they will produce another productive meeting.

Suppose you just had a successful meeting during which a group of regional managers got together and worked out some guidelines for a new bonus system that addressed the difficult problem of rewarding fairly everyone involved in achieving a large sale. If the work that those managers put in is ignored, any attempt to repeat the success of the last meeting would be likely to fail. If, however, it was pursued, then the next meeting starts off with built-in enthusiasm. Success generates the desire for more success.

The first step in building a bridge is to establish which side of the river you currently are on. In other words, if you identify too much paperwork as being an obstacle to effective after-sale service, that's your current side of the river. Then you decide where you want to go. Perhaps you want to eliminate fifty percent of your organization's paperwork by the next meeting and address the elimination of a further twenty-five percent at the meeting itself.

The third step is to plan all of the steps in building the crossing. You might decide to list all the forms that have to be filled out and collect opinions on what should be eliminated, simplified, combined, or retained.

As the construction gets underway, you test it out. In other words, once a few forms have been eliminated, you question everyone affected, including outsiders, to see if there are any bad side effects. If there are, you adapt immediately.

While these changes are being put into practice everyone should be kept up to date on what is being accomplished now and how that will relate to what will be done during the next meeting. Before the meeting, you should prepare a year-end report, identifying areas that still need to be addressed, for the original group that identified the problem.

When you are bridging between meetings, your goals become easier to achieve because you're basing them on past experience. It's much easier to learn new information if it's related to information previously known. Meetings can continue, with related themes, over a period of years, linked in between by follow-up activities. I was engaged by a company to produce a series of meetings, the objective of which was to make the managers of a chain of restaurants more innovative and aggressive as well as more sensitive to their role in the success of the company. We decided to run a series of three meetings over a period of three years, in order to introduce certain ideas progressively.

I've already referred to the first two of these meetings which had the themes "Reach for the Top" and "Rise above the Rest." Both were pointing toward the third year which had the theme "Search for the Key." That meeting answered the question "How do I reach for the top and rise above the rest?" The answer was that you search within yourself to find the strength and desire to overcome obstacles.

Between the first and second meetings, we ran a retail customer-service program, stressing the key idea of people-oriented store management. There were monthly newsletters as well as videocassettes with messages from the president and the keynote speaker.

Between the second and third meetings, we continued the videocassettes and added quarterly store visits from senior executives and the guest speaker who had addressed the second meeting. We also added a large financial award for the best performing store as well as "Quality of Service" awards judged by the store managers themselves with such prizes as cash bonuses, department store credits, and home furnishings.

A bridging program must be flexible and amenable to change in response to changes in services, programs, markets, products, and people. Unlike a real bridge over a real river, the direction of a bridge between meetings can change, because the direction in which a company is headed might change. The important thing, however, is that the bridge does lead *somewhere.*

I once put on a meeting for an association of forest engineering firms. During the previous meeting, the association had identified a problem involving expensive heavy equipment that was breaking down too often. The intent had been to follow up that meeting by finding ways to reduce downtime.

The upcoming meeting was to be a training forum for teaching the new repair methods. However, in the interval a new problem arose involving an influx of new foreign competitors for the association members and a constantly changing government policy regarding the foreign competition. In planning the upcoming meeting, we had to keep tabs on this new issue on a daily basis in case we had to change the theme of the meeting to deal with it instead of the repair problems. As it turned out, the competition problem resolved itself and we continued on as planned. Had we needed to, however, we were prepared to bridge effectively to either issue.

You can't have a twelve-month bridge between meetings. It has to be broken down into individual months or quarters. The message and enthusiasm of the past meeting has to get a booster shot during each period.

The best way to do that is to give people a good incentive to continue to remember and use the message and information they received. In the follow-up to "Rise above the Rest," the monthly videocassettes included regular updates on the quality-of-service award program, publicizing the winners and praising those who had improved their performance. We kept reinforcing the objectives of the program and the original theme of the meeting.

Grouping for Action

People will do a lot more when they are working with colleagues than when they are working by themselves. If someone is alone, kicking a ball around on a field, there's not much incentive for him or her to exert much effort. But put that individual into a serious game of touch football and he or she will put out. If not, the team will probably lose and that individual will hear about it from his or her teammates. People want to be respected and valued by their co-workers and they'll work hard to earn that respect.

Furthermore, the cliche that "two heads are better than one" is true more often than not. A group of people interrelating among themselves is more productive than individuals acting alone. That's the power of synergy, and you can capture that power by putting people into groups as part of the follow-up to your meeting.

It's important that the groups be small and that the emphasis be on the positive. I don't like to emphasize competition between the follow-up groups because someone always loses and that introduces an unwanted negative element.

Always select follow-up groups before the large meeting starts, not after it's over. This should be done on the basis of the audience research carried out before the meeting so that appropriate follow-up groups are chosen. These groups, which worked together during the meeting, continue working together in the follow-up activities after the meeting.

There might be, for example, a communications group, a project group, and a sales group. Each group could have a name — the Montreal Canadiens, the Chicago Cubs, or whatever. That gives them an identity and a personality and helps group members to develop loyalty.

The communications systems provided for the groups should be both accessible and rapid. I did a grouping project as a follow-up to a meeting for a transportation company. There were three groups. One was working on regional sales problems, another on implementation of a new computer system to improve the scheduling of trucks, and the third was working on after-sales follow-up and implementation of sales skills demonstrated at the meeting.

To help the groups with any problems, we provided an 800–number so that when anyone needed information or advice, he or she could call and get it instantly. A newsletter or a computer network can fulfill the same function.

Natural leaders will emerge in each group and that's something that should be encouraged. There may be some resentment but it will fade away and be replaced by a sense of solidarity if the leader is capable. Each group needs a leader because without one there will be too many opinions and not enough decisions. The emergence of these leaders is to the organization's long-term benefit because it's a way to identify those who are going to lead the organization itself in the future.

Military leaders for centuries have been aware of the usefulness of grouping. Armies everywhere encourage regimental loyalties. The regiments are competitive, one against the other, but they are all members of the same army and they have a tremendous pride in it. That combination — competition, cooperation, and pride — is a potent force for transforming the motivation you achieved in your meeting into results in the real world.

Fueling the Follow-up Engine

Incentives and motivators are the fuel that powers the follow-up engine. It's much easier to keep people enthusiastic during a three-day meeting than it is to keep them up throughout the months that follow. An exhortation that fires them up during the meeting quickly loses its force when repeated over and over.

Incentives give people a personal reason to stay involved. They are a way of creating successes for people. Everybody on a soccer team can't score a goal in every game. So what keeps the players motivated? The incentive of competing for the championship at the end of the season. When the team captain lifts the championship trophy in celebration, everyone on the team shares in the triumph.

In sports, however, there are always losers. Not so in an organization's incentive program, which can be designed to ensure that everyone is a winner.

The greatest single incentive is self-esteem. People can move mountains if they believe in themselves and others believe in them too. Our creativity and skills come from our feelings of our own value. When we have good reason to believe in that value, we try harder and produce more.

Money isn't the best incentive. It's spent quickly, sometimes even before it's received. Tangible rewards should be in the form of gifts such as stereo sets, video cameras, or trips.

All competition for incentives must be fair and everybody should have an equal chance to win. If people begin to feel that they're too far behind to win — or too far ahead to lose — they'll slow down. You'll have a demotivator instead of a motivator. This means that adjustments have to be made for those who start at a disadvantage. For example, one salesperson might have a territory with many rich and faithful customers while another has a territory full of hard, demanding customers. You can't set the same standards for both.

An incentive system should reward the behaviors that you want to encourage. You have to be able to identify those behaviors and aim your incentives directly at them. Perhaps you have some warehouse employees whose time-management skills need upgrading. You want them to maximize the amount of inventory they can move in one shift. The reward should be for best performance in terms of goods moved per hour. Offer help with any other behaviors that might need it but base the rewards on the key time-management behavior.

Many incentive programs fail to identify critical behaviors. They reward some type of an objective, such as achieving a total dollar sales figure; the first person to reach it is the winner. Then everyone stops doing the critical behavior.

Your incentive should be fine-tuned and precisely targeted. Suppose the critical behavior you wanted to encourage was prospecting new customers, which may mean cold-calling. You should reward cold-calling and the results obtained from it. If you simply reward the highest amount earned, most people will go to existing clients and squeeze a few more sales out of them, rather than developing new clients.

It's important to have a balance between tangible rewards such as a new car or a trip to Hawaii and intangible, emotional rewards. The winner of an expensive trip is going to be thrilled. But once it's over, he or she is back at the same old grind. But if the tangible reward is combined with such intangibles as the acknowledgement of his or her peers and the thanks of the organization, the effects will be long-lasting.

Incentives shouldn't be once-only affairs. They should be built into the year, in a series of peaks, each one a little larger than the last. It all culminates at your meeting when a whole new program is launched.

The element of fun and excitement should never be lost. We devised an incentive program based on a meeting for a manufacturer of lighting products and batteries. The object of the meeting and of the incentive program that followed was generating new clients. The incentive program was called "The Treasure Within." Each time an individual got a new client he or she received a new piece of a treasure map. Each map was different to prevent people from collaborating in the search for treasure. When the map was completed the holder could follow it and find the buried treasure, which included VCRs, video cameras, the keys to a car, and $10,000 in gold.

The program ran for six months and the place was abuzz with excitement the whole time. The excitement built steadily as the treasure maps came closer to completion. There were more treasure maps than winners but even incompleted maps won some kind of prize as well as receiving bonus points as a head start toward the next year's competition.

Action Plans and Support Structures

You want your people to use what they learned in the meeting over the year that follows. In devising an action plan to achieve this goal, make sure that the time frames are realistic. If people are given too little time, they can't achieve a goal and if they have too much time, they'll achieve it and then lose interest.

Standards for determining whether a goal is reached should be quantifiable. If the goal is identifying one hundred new prospective customers in five months, then the goal is twenty prospects a month. Having quantifiable standards allows participants to measure their progress. If they're behind target, they know how much harder they have to work. If they're ahead, perhaps they can reduce the time allotted for reaching that particular goal and use that extra time for something else.

A support structure is necessary for a follow-up campaign. An important part of that structure is the mentor — someone empowered to assign responsibilities, act as a source of information, and dispense rewards. If people are off base, the mentor can step in and suggest that they redirect themselves.

A problem-solving mechanism also is required. In one follow-up, we had a problem-solving committee whose job was to review specific selling situations for a new piece of printing equipment that was being sold to hard-nosed, skeptical industry buyers. The committee was made up of senior sales executives, friendly clients, the marketing director, and design engineers. People could call an 800– number and explain their problem. A member of the committee would do some investigation and come up with possible solutions or strategies. The committee members didn't always come up with the solution the first time but they would persist and were able to solve most of the problems.

Teamwork is yet another support structure. It is particularly valuable when a problem has many different aspects. The goal of turning up one hundred new sales prospects, for example, involves market research, selling skills, telemarketing, direct mail, and after-sales service. A team formed of specialists in each of these areas would be well qualified to address the problem.

Curiously, one of the benefits of bringing people together in teams is that problems that weren't apparent when people were operating separately, come to the fore once people are in teams. Often an entirely different problem will emerge as a result of the interaction of the ideas, insights, and special backgrounds of the follow-up team members. This is a good thing because you can't solve a problem unless you know it's there.

Suppose a team has been formed to plan the installation of some new machinery. The operator on the team is able to inform the engineer that the comfort of the operators has been overlooked. Together, they may discover a new issue that had been overlooked before.

Follow-up Feedback

In order to know that the follow-up program is working, a feedback system is needed. Unless monitoring is carried out to assess whether the objectives sought during the meeting are being realized, there is no way of knowing whether you're getting any payoff on your investment.

Measuring something in a quantitative way produces straightforward feedback. Either the salesperson got twenty new customers or he or she didn't. Goals may have to be adjusted, depending on what happens. The reality of the marketplace may be that the goals are too high. On the other hand, they may be too low and they can be increased.

Qualities are harder to measure than quantities. How can someone's satisfaction with his or her employer be measured? How can confidence, trust, belief in a philosophy, dedication, caring be measured? The only way is through an intuitive reading of people. What makes the assessment particularly hard is that many people are used to hiding their feelings; they feel threatened when these feelings are exposed. But the experienced manager develops sharp antennae.

As part of the feedback effort, the follow-up coordinator should establish networks of individuals to report on whether the desired objectives are being met. Some should share the coordinator's values and assumptions and some should be critical of them; both kinds of feedback are valuable.

Suppose a meeting has been held on the theme "Training Is the Road to Better Sales." The follow-up coordinator should ask the individuals in the network for an appraisal of people's attitudes to training. Are managers being asked to devise in-house courses? Are people signing up in greater numbers for courses that already exist? Channels of communication should be set up — letters, telephone calls, personal visits — and those channels should be kept operating. The people in your network must be made aware of how much their help is valued; otherwise they'll stop offering it.

The coordinator will have to develop a technique for analyzing the information acquired through feedback. As this book is about meetings, not management theory, I won't go into detail on this point. The coordinator will know which techniques are available and choose those that are suitable.

At this point, the follow-up coordinator is ready to report the findings to management. Some people shy away from this step because of a fear of failure. That's a mistake. Encourage your staff not to be afraid of failure, but to use it. If the feedback indicates that something is being done incorrectly, it can be changed. And it's best if such problems surface early in the follow-up process rather than later, which is why monitoring is so important.

Swinging into the Next Event

With the information derived from the follow-up program, it shouldn't be hard to create a link between your last meeting, the follow-up activities that succeeded it, and the meeting that's coming up.

In baseball, a team that just misses winning the pennant in the stretch drive takes solace from having been through an invaluable learning process. "Now we know how to win," the losing players say.

That should be your attitude. What you should strive to avoid is falling victim to disassociation, or the tendency to break off associations with a past event as that event recedes into history. People will tend to forget the message and call to action that came out of a meeting that happened ten months ago. Your follow-up program works against that tendency. Your teaser campaign for the next meeting, invoking a theme that carries last year's a step forward, also helps to reinforce what was learned last year.

Active involvement by the attendees in the outcome of one meeting leads to success in the subsequent meeting. I organized a conference to help introduce a computerized inventory system for an office supplies company. Enthusiasm for the project was high throughout the ranks of the company because the new system could improve delivery times and customer service in general.

But in the year following the meeting, one problem after another developed in the new system. The prevailing attitude became one of grim determination to make the thing work because, despite all the hassles, its value was unquestioned. Yet there were widespread complaints about the lack of time for dealing with the problems.

The theme of the first meeting had been "A Step into the Future." We decided that the next year's event should be entitled "The Future Is Now." It dealt with three areas. The first was the development of solution teams to create time for solving the ongoing problems. The second was a list of unresolved bugs to be brainstormed during the meeting. The third was a commitment by all levels of management to resolve the problems.

The second meeting successfully rekindled enthusiasm for the automation project and from that point on, implementation of the system went much more smoothly. The lesson is that one meeting can't solve everything. A meeting never stands alone. It must be integrated into the business year and linked to the next year's meeting. Follow-up is a process that never ends.

8

RUNNING THE EVENT

Once you, the senior executive, have decided the meeting strategy and assembled the planning team that produces the concepts, the meeting coordinator begins the massive task of turning these concepts into reality. Although you will not be directly involved in this part of the process, you will need to be aware of the outcomes of the various stages. While the following two chapters are addressed directly to meeting coordinators, it will help you to see the steps that are followed and to identify the desired results.

Rule Number One for meeting coordinators is: Be people-conscious. Meeting coordinators tend to be detail-oriented and with good reason; there are, after all, hundreds of details to worry about. The logistics of a major meeting are endless. It's natural that the first thing you will want to do on your arrival at the hotel will be to check whether the hotel staff has provided all the items you requested and whether the menus are on the tables for the opening banquet.

These details will be easier to resolve if you never forget that you are dealing with people. The banquet manager may have had a bad day. Or maybe he's indifferent because he knows that meetings aren't a big money maker for the hotel. Or what you consider inadequate attention to your needs may be simply a reflection of your meeting's status as only one of dozens of things he has to do that day. Try to keep his problems in mind and don't treat him or any of the hotel's staff like underlings: "Hey, you" "Do this" "Get over here." That sort of attitude can trigger a lot of resentment; it's definitely not in your self-interest.

I once ran a meeting that required a great amount of cooperation from the hotel staff. We had a 16,000-square foot (1500-m²)
meeting room precisely laid out to accommodate a variety of
delicate machinery and complex arrangements of video screens
and computers. It was vital that each piece of equipment be in
the right place at the right time.

Unfortunately, the coordinator who was working with me at
the time didn't understand human relations. His idea of getting
the staff to do what he wanted was to bark orders at them. That's
an excellent method of persuading people to work less, rather
than more, efficiently. Which is exactly what happened.

The result was that we started half an hour late, an inexcus-
able delay. Meetings must start on time; if they don't, people get
bored and restless and the event is lurching out of your control
before you've even begun. This bad experience taught me a valuable lesson — the most important part of running the event is
being conscious of the people who are helping you.

It also taught me that grace under pressure is the prime
attribute of the successful coordinator. Being under pressure is
no excuse for being rude. A coordinator is always under pressure,
yet despite the pressure, a good coordinator doesn't blow up. He
or she gets things done by being gracious and understanding.

People-consciousness doesn't stop with the hotel staff. If you
treat the attendees as a cowboy would treat a herd of cattle, you
run the risk of triggering an outbreak of resentment and boredom. Trying to produce an upbeat, motivational atmosphere
while your audience is feeling boredom, anger, and resentment
is like swimming upstream; the current of the meeting is against
you.

I remember a meeting for five hundred salespeople of high-
technology equipment. These highly paid individuals were
cramped into one small room. It wasn't long before the complaints began to flow. "These chairs are uncomfortable." "The
water isn't cold." "The pencils aren't sharp." "I can't see the
screen." "I can't hear the speaker." Yet the meeting was a good
one. Both the speaker and the audio-visuals were excellent. But
because the attendees were so annoyed by the poor accommodation and minor discomforts, they were in no mood to appreciate
anything.

If you treat people like cattle you will frustrate those who are
truly involved and excited about the program. They want more
time to absorb what they've just heard and to talk about it some

more, and you're trying to push them out the door to another session. They're dying to ask the guest speaker a question and you're insisting that time's up. I know that I've preached the importance of agendas, scheduling, and being on time, but a skillful coordinator has to anticipate the way the audience will react. Because he or she has researched the audience well and knows what the guest speaker is going to say, adequate time can be allotted in the schedule for questions. You must plan enough open and free discussion that the meeting moves along from one item on the agenda to the next, at an efficient yet civilized pace.

The key to moving large groups of people around without angering them is to have the routes well marked beforehand. Perhaps you can lay the routes out with rope dividers. But don't just assume that the hotel will do it; you have to arrange it. Or suppose you have five hundred people in a large meeting room watching an audio-visual. After the presentation is over, they are going to break up into smaller sessions in other parts of the hotel. You should inform the attendees beforehand that they are going to break up into groups and you should have people on hand to guide them. A ratio of one guide to twenty-five people is ideal. The maximum that one guide can handle effectively is thirty-five people.

You must leave lots of time for all of this to happen. A group of five hundred will need half an hour to assemble into several subgroups in different places. They are not all going to move at the same rate. Instill in your guides the need to treat the attendees with courtesy. Not "Move over...come on...hurry up" but "Would everyone be kind enough to assemble here, please? Thank you very much. We will be going to Conference Room C...."

Sometimes a state of general unhappiness invades a meeting. It's a peculiar phenomenon. It only takes a few people with gripes — "I don't like this city" "My wife said the spouses' program was terrible" "I hated having to use the subway to get to that event" and so on — and before long the contagion spreads. Everyone else finds something to complain about. A good way to trigger such a mass reaction is to herd people about without taking account of their individuality.

If this atmosphere does set in, try to identify the leaders. People tend to follow the example of the most outspoken and aggressive of their peers. When you've identified the ringleader, try to deal with his or her complaints, carefully and politely but not defensively. Some of the complaints may well be legitimate and you should try to enlist the complainer into helping you devise solutions. You can say something like, "Look, this may be a legitimate point. How would you suggest we resolve it? I really don't have the answer myself."

Don't be unwilling to apologize if that's appropriate, by saying something like, "I'm sorry, that was a mistake, let's get it solved right away." At that point, you'll probably get a positive response when you ask the individual not to complain in front of the others. "Let's try to keep this event upbeat," you say. "I know there's a problem. But let's be positive. Could you help me?"

If you do promise to resolve a problem, get back to the complainer within the hour if possible. Otherwise, he or she will complain even louder.

Gauging Energy Levels and Gaining Commitment

The more people there are at a meeting, the higher the energy level is. The coordinator should be alert to the energy level of the audience because that energy level is one of his or her best allies. Properly manipulated, it can allow the meeting to carry itself. Some coordinators notice that people seem a bit low and think, "Oh my God, things are starting to die. I'd better whip up some action." But if you understand the ebb and flow of energy levels, and play those levels properly, the meeting takes on a life of its own.

As the coordinator, you can measure the energy level of your audience by strolling among the attendees and talking to them. An audience with a low energy level is in a wait-and-see mood: people are waiting to see what the meeting offers them before they commit their energy to it. A medium energy level indicates people are devoting the same energy to this event as they do to their everyday jobs. They are prepared to be involved — but not too involved. A high energy level indicates a heightened degree of interest in the content of the meeting and a willingness to participate actively in the proceedings.

It's possible to predict when different energy levels will occur. If you've done a good pre-meeting advertising job, then energy levels will be high at the start. If you haven't, energy that would otherwise have been spent on cooperating and participating will be wasted as the attendees try to figure out what's going on. A disorganized or late start to a meeting can also cannibalize the energy your attendees bring with them. If things aren't working out well, they'll fall into the wait-and-see mood. "I'd better see what's happening here," they'll say to themselves. "I'd better hold off and figure things out."

But no matter how well you've advertised and how well organized you are, energy levels will drop off before and after lunch. Then, the levels will go up again around 6 or 7 p.m., when the day's agenda is over and people are anticipating the evening's events.

Because energy levels are high first thing in the morning, that's a good time to demand commitment from your audience. I did a sales meeting for a computer company on the theme "You've Got That Magic Touch," the name of a song. First thing in the morning, we put on a fifties-style rock band that got the meeting off to a roaring, high energy start that lasted all day.

Too often this high energy period is wasted on boring speeches by otherwise sincere but inept speakers. Far better to use it for a powerful audio-visual or an inspirational speaker and put the other speeches on afterward. But never schedule a poor speaker for just before lunch. The attendees' energy level is naturally low then and a dull speech brings them down even farther. It gives them the feeling that the meeting is over and they'll just coast the rest of the way.

Before lunch, I like to schedule a statement or action plan about what will be happening after lunch. The plan includes reasons and payoffs for getting involved. These have included such deluxe incentives as keys to a Porsche for the most active attendee as well as treasure chests full of silver dollars. Prizes are a most effective way to get people's attention.

Being sensitive to energy levels means being flexible. You should always be prepared to realign some of the elements in the meeting to coincide with energy levels. If energy is low, you might decide to have the business game now instead of in two hours. Suppose your audience has just suffered through a boring presentation of facts and figures. Why not insert an interactive open panel into the schedule? Put marketing people on the panel who can answer the attendees' questions. The panel could be held during lunch or outside if you're at a resort. It's a way of recapturing the sense of involvement that was dissipated by the dull speaker.

The goal in designing a meeting is to get the attendees committed to the objectives you have set. As with energy, there are three levels of commitment. There are the low-level, wait-and-see folks. Then there are the medium-commitment types who are involved but waiting to hear more before they get really involved. The high-commitment people are those bent on learning as much as they can and who identify with the objectives that the meeting has set.

The best way to get people committed to a goal, and to measure their degree of commitment, is to ask them to stand up and be counted. I mean this literally. Suppose your company is an airline that has recently changed its name and revised its business strategy. On an intellectual level, people might agree that the change makes sense. But real commitment requires doing something. You can't go out and start selling in a meeting but you can stand up and be counted.

Ask people to stand and indicate their level of commitment. What do they think of the change and what will their commitment lead them to do when the meeting is over? That physical action of actually standing up and speaking solidifies the commitment. They can't back down after doing that.

Concentrate on getting the medium-commitment people to stand up and be counted. They are the ones who are most open to positive change. If you are operating group workshops or discussions, insert committed people into the medium-commitment group.

As for the low-commitment types, I once had success by grouping them together for a discussion with the company executives. The executives were told beforehand to listen to what these people were saying and not to put anybody down. It was most productive. Some still wouldn't commit but a few became highly committed and many adopted the medium-commitment position.

Overcoming Murphy's Law

Everything is in place, everyone has arrived, and the meeting is in progress. So how can you prevent things from going wrong? You can't. But you can be prepared to deal with problems as they arise. To become effective at doing that, a coordinator has to get into the habit of trying to predict the future. This is not done with a crystal ball, but by making use of what he or she knows from experience.

Suppose you're coordinating a banquet for a hundred and fifty people. What can go wrong? Food poisoning? Someone choking on food? A heart attack? Probably none of these things will happen but there's no guarantee that they won't. You've got to be prepared: it is mandatory that you have a doctor on call. That may seem obvious but an effective coordinator attends carefully to all details, including the obvious ones.

People are people, not angels. You've got to be ready to deal with bad behavior. I recall a meeting for a soft drink company at which the husband of one of the secretaries downed quite a few too many drinks and became verbally abusive to the president of the company. He tried to throw a punch at him but was wrestled to the ground before he could connect.

His wife was so ashamed that she never came back to work at that company although her superiors urged her to return. The sad thing is that it could have been avoided because the man's drunkenness had been apparent. He had been demanding, for example, to have a private room where he could serve drinks to his friends. We could have arranged that or, better still, for a taxi to take him home.

Since that experience, I always arrange for a private room — I call them "sobering rooms." If someone becomes drunk and disruptive, you or a team member should invite the individual there with an offer of more drinks, if that's what he or she wants, or coffee. The important thing is to get the person out of harm's way.

If the service at your banquet is slow, people might get impatient. What do you do if a hundred and fifty people start banging their spoons on the table? I once had to alter an agenda quickly to calm an impatient crowd. We brought on our after-dinner act — a comedienne dressed up as a Martian. She was a big hit and the crowd stopped worrying about the slow service.

If you don't have any Martians on hand, how about samples of a new product your company is bringing out, or an information kit? Either one would serve to distract people's attention for a few minutes until the food finally arrives. Overcoming Murphy's Law means being prepared.

During one meeting — not, I'm glad to say, one of mine — the theme of "Shoot Straight" was illustrated by a couple of characters dressed up as gunfighters who sauntered into the banquet room wielding .38-caliber pistols. They promptly began to shoot the place up — with blanks. These "bullets" themselves weren't lethal but two elderly executives were so surprised that they suffered cardiac stress and had to be rushed to hospital. Happily, both of them survived. A planner conscious of Murphy's Law wouldn't have staged a surprise gunfight even if everyone in the room had been checked out for heart ailments or stress-related conditions.

During one meeting, I had a couple of pirates on stage. They got into a dispute and began duelling. On came the pirate captain who raised his pistol. He raised it slowly so that everyone knew what was coming and no one was severely startled when he fired the gun. The captain then became the host of a business game. All of which proves that it's possible to use the element of surprise and have fun without scaring your audience half to death.

The basic principle is to foresee the worst possible outcome as well as the best. I have already described this process as "Murphy's Law Antidote." Champion athletes use a similar technique to prepare for competition. They call it "visualization." Daley Thompson, the British athlete who has won the Olympic decathlon twice, spends several days before a major event lying down and imagining himself overcoming every possible obstacle that might occur in competition. In the Los Angeles Olympics of 1984, Thompson missed his first two tries in the pole vault. But he easily cleared the bar on his third and final attempt. Because he had mentally rehearsed being in exactly that predicament — and winning — he didn't panic. He was mentally prepared to give his best effort when he needed it.

This technique can be usefully applied to almost any aspect of life. I consider it a fundamental part of the successful coordinator's arsenal. Here's an example of how it might work. Suppose you're running a business game as a postbanquet entertainment and you have a wheel of fortune, a master of ceremonies, a podium, spotlights, and music. And of course you have a set of questions and answers because that's what the game is about: the contestants will be asked questions and the one who gets the most right will win.

First, you define the nature of the occasion — a form of entertainment. You hope people will enjoy it, that they'll be surprised because they hadn't expected it, and that they will learn something relevant to their roles in your organization from the questions and answers.

Next, you identify potential problems. Based on your experience, what's the best-case and worst-case scenario? What can go wrong? One thing that can go wrong is that someone becomes embarrassed. Once we ran a business game at a meeting attended by people from a variety of ethnic backgrounds. For cultural reasons, some of them didn't like to be up on stage. Their command of English wasn't good and the whole experience had a negative impact.

The Murphy's Law Antidote is to check beforehand to find out if some people in your audience object to, or would be uncomfortable with, that sort of exposure. You can design your game to keep these people off the stage. In one case, we handed cards out to everyone and made sure that people of a certain background got an ace. The host had been warned not to choose anyone with an ace. It worked smoothly and no one was any the wiser.

Suppose the host of the business game starts telling off-color jokes that wind up offending a large part of the audience? Chances are it never occurred to you that a professional who works business meetings could be so dumb. Murphy's Law, as I know from experience, proves otherwise. You have to practice prevention by making sure that the host, just like your guest speakers, is fully aware of the nature of your audience and of what sort of material is appropriate.

The worst-case scenario is that, despite your best efforts, the host launches into an obscene monologue. You and your team should be prepared for such eventualities. If the host is running a game, you could have someone slip him or her a note along with the questions to be asked, telling him or her to cool it. Or you could make sure you know in advance how to cut the power to the microphone.

What are you going to do about sessions that run too long? Watch for natural breaks. Perhaps a coffee break is coming up or it's the end of the hour. You stand up and say, "OK, ladies and gentlemen, it's three o'clock. I think it's time we had a short break. When we come back we're going to have an open discussion."

What if you've got a problem with attendees persistently refusing to return to the meeting from coffee breaks? Place some of your team members at the phones, the stairs to the lobby, and other key points. Have them announce, "The meeting is resuming in two minutes, you had better hurry up please." You will always have stragglers, but if you use this technique persistently, you can minimize their numbers.

Suppose you're holding a meeting in mid-July in the midst of a heat wave. Murphy's Law states that the air-conditioning system will break down and the hotel will be unable to get it repaired until after your meeting is over. Farfetched? Perhaps. But disasters do happen and it's your responsibility to be prepared for them.

If you are in a resort, you can hold the meeting outside. You say you're using audio-visuals? No problem. Set up your equipment on the lawns and show the audio-visuals at night. I've done that by choice, not because of a disaster, and people found it exciting.

If you are in the city, you should always have an alternate meeting site available, whether or not it's midsummer. Movie theaters that aren't open for matinees are your best bet. I once booked a theater to show some commercials to a group. It was such a comfortable and pleasant atmosphere that we stayed much longer than planned. You pay the union projectionist the standard rate plus a bonus and allow the theater to sell popcorn to your attendees. That makes everybody happy.

Keeping Track of Details

You've made your basic plans, tried to predict glitches, and done your preventative and remedial planning. Now you can check it all against reality. One of your most important activities as a coordinator is making notes. Everything should be registered, although not necessarily recorded in detail. If something bad happens, even a small problem, make a note of it. If something good happens, and some item works out far better than expected, make a note of it. If an idea occurs to you about how an event might be improved, make a note of it. If service at the banquet was too hurried, write it down. This is how you improve your ability to run meetings.

Your planning team has produced a flowchart that breaks the meeting into its parts (see Figure 5-1, page 73 for sample and a step-by-step outline of flowchart scheduling). It can be in chronological or any other logical order. If it's in order of priority, certain tasks will take precedence even though, chronologically, they don't happen until later in the schedule. For instance, people won't move into their hotel rooms until just before the meeting begins, but booking those rooms is one of the first things you do.

A typical flowchart might describe a six-month process, starting from your first steps in designing the meeting and ending with follow-up activities. Break these six months down into weeks. Then break each section into steps. The steps are of two types: items that can be delegated and those that can't. How many napkins are going to be on each table? That decision can be delegated. How many tables are going to be in the room so that everybody can be seated comfortably? That's your decision. How many guest speakers will address the meeting? That's your decision. Which rooms will they stay in? That decision can be delegated.

You should do a best-case/worst-case analysis to decide how long you will need to make each decision. There are a great many decisions to be made: the final design of a theme logo, the actual meeting dates, the final menus. If you're lucky, the planning team can make Decision X in a day or two. But if the mails are slow and somebody's pet cat dies, it might take two weeks. These things usually average out. Two days plus two weeks is sixteen days, so you can confidently give yourselves eight days to make Decision X. You note the point on your flowchart at which the decision should be made and at that time you check that indeed this has been done.

The chart identifies connections between decision or delegation points and other decision or delegation points. For instance, you have to decide on the shape and number of tables on March 17 but you also have to decide on the color of the tablecloths. Once you've decided on round tables, you're in a position to choose the tablecloths.

The time line running along the top of the flowchart tells you at a glance how you are progressing. Are you ahead of time or behind time? If the chart shows you that your audio-visual script was to be approved by January 15 and it's now January 18 and it's not approved, then you'd better put some pressure on.

Put all major agreements between yourself and your suppliers in writing. In addition to your letter of agreement with the hotel, you also should have written agreements with the audio-visual producer, the person who is bringing the rubber chickens for the skit that you're planning, and the premiums and incentives supplier. (The latter is also known as the trinkets-and-trash supplier — the company that provides the pens, cups, writing pads, and buttons found at every meeting.) The letter of agreement needn't be long (see Figure 8–1). It should simply set out what is being supplied, at what cost, and on what delivery date, and be signed by both parties.

Figure 8–1 Hotel Management Letter of Agreement

Dear _____

We are using your facilities during the period _____ to _____ for our _____ conference. Since much of the success of our event depends on you, we would like to share with you our specific needs so that you can be fully prepared to service us.

The following is a complete list of requirements in terms of materials, supplies, and services that will be used during our conference. If you have any problems meeting these requirements, please contact us as soon as possible so that remedies can be effected. Otherwise, please sign this agreement and return a copy to us by June 17.

1. All participants to have conference materials placed in their rooms by hotel personnel.
2. Meeting room (The Windows) to have two (2) flip charts by 7:00 p.m. on September 17.
3. Each table to have eight (8) tent cards placed on them by 7:00 p.m. on September 17.
4. Six (6) staging risers to be placed at north end of meeting room by 7:00 p.m. September 17.
5. Banquet manager to be available up to 9:00 p.m., September 17; 6:00 p.m., September 18 and 19; and 12:00 p.m. September 20.
6. Hotel safe to be made available from 5:00 p.m., September 17 to 7:00 p.m., September 20.
7. Area near front desk to be set aside for lost and found articles.
8. Table (2' x 4') to be set up in front of The Windows by 7:00 p.m., September 17.
9. Four (4) chairs to be set up around table by 7:00 p.m., September 17.

Agreed upon price of _____ .

Your cooperation in this matter is greatly appreciated.

Signed: _____

Meeting Coordinator

_____

Hotel Management

If the planning team hasn't already done so, you should prepare checklists (see Figure 8–2) for each aspect of the meeting. Lists are different from flowcharts in that the latter show the relationships between different parts of the meeting without including every last detail. On the other hand, your separate checklist for a one-minute song-and-dance number might have a dozen or more items on it. You tick the items off as they are dealt with. There should be room on the list for comment in case something has changed or you want to add something.

Figure 8–2 Hotel Checklist

ITEM	GROUP RESPONSIBLE	COORDINATOR	DONE
1. Ice sculptures for banquet	Banquet manager	J. Sandler	☐
2. Kosher food caterer	Catering manager	D. Shelby	☐
3. Popcorn wagon	Our team	P. Sullivan	☐
4. Silver tableware	Banquet manager	J. Sandler	☐
5. Cocktail music combo	Our team	A. Thompson	☐
6. Place-card holders	Catering manager	D. Shelby	☐
7. Flowers on tables	Banquet manager	J. Sandler	☐
8. Audio-visual equipment	Our team	R. Wasley	☐
9. Limousines at door	Our team	K. Zerkles	☐
10. Piper for entrance	Our team	B. Cockburn	☐
11. Gifts at each table	Our team	D. Donnell	☐
12. Head table seating	Our team	D. Donnell	☐
13. Registration kits set up	Our team	K. Zerkles	☐
14. Name tags in rooms	Our team	K. Zerkles	☐
15. Baggage holding room	Concierge	W. Lamonde	☐
16. Maps of subway in rooms	Our team	K. Zerkles	☐
17. Simultaneous interpreters	Our team	D. Sullivan	☐
18. Room layout (seating)	Catering manager	D. Shelby	☐
19. Room layout (staging)	Our team	R. Wasley	☐
20. Room decor	Our team	K. Zerkles	☐
21. Roped-off areas	Our team	R. King	☐
22. Meals for technical crews	Our team	R. King	☐
23. Liaison with union	Our team	R. King	☐
24. Rehearsal coordination	Our team	K. Zerkles	☐
25. Breakout room direction signs	Our team	K. Zerkles	☐
26. Lost and found contact	Concierge	W. Lamonde	☐
27. Welcome booth at front door	Our team	R. King	☐
28. Hostesses for seating, etc.	Our team	R. King	☐
29. Pick-up by tour buses on day one	Our team	R. King	☐
30. Valuables put in hotel safe	Concierge	W. Lamonde	☐

Your lists, flowcharts, and letters of agreement should be with you during the meeting. If there's a problem with the hotel, you whip out your letter and point out what the hotel had agreed to do and request politely that it proceed to do it. Most often, the hotel employee will apologize, saying that he or she didn't realize what had been agreed. Hotel staff like having everything in black and white. Coordinators should too because it makes for successful meetings.

The Art of Delegation

The people to whom you delegate tasks must be trustworthy. You have to trust that they will check the menus as they are supposed to, that they will greet people at the airport, arrange the limousines, and deal with the baggage problems. The worst thing you can do to one of these people is to assign him or her to be a jack-of-all-trades. Your instruction should be, "You're in charge of all ground transportation." Don't add, "Oh and there will be other things as well but I don't know what they are right now." That's no good because it leaves your team member up in the air.

Choose people you know you can work with and that you know can do the job. Don't choose someone just because he or she is available. If you do, you might be choosing a problem. During your pre-meeting coordination, meet with your team at the beginning of each week. Find out what people have done, what they're going to do, and what they need to help them do it. That weekly meeting brings everyone up to date and launches the coordination process for the following week. It's useful too because it brings everyone together. For instance, Bill, who is planning the menu, may need some advice about wine; it may well be that Joan, your transportation chief, has a friend who is a wine expert.

As this weekly process continues, insist that your team members voice every problem but that each problem be accompanied by a recommended solution. Not "My God, I can't get along with the audio-visual producer, what do I do?" "I can't get along with the audio-visual producer. I suggest we get someone else" is much better even if the proposed solution is not feasible, because it gets your people thinking in terms of problem solution. Finding problems is easy; solving them isn't. A problem-solving mentality is essential if you're to achieve your goal of keeping the coordination process moving. If you solve a week's worth of problems and raise a week's worth of new challenges, you'll do just fine.

Well before the meeting starts, you have to appoint someone who can keep the ship afloat and on course if a health problem or some other emergency causes your absence. Your second-in-command should be like yourself — level-headed, practical, quick-thinking, energetic, well-liked by his or her colleagues, and capable of handling authority.

It's your responsibility to keep your second-in-command well informed on everything you have done. A good way to do that is to have a blueprint — a binder containing all the details of the meeting. It should be divided into categories such as transportation, accommodation, registration, communications. These categories are further subdivided: for example, communications is divided into such items as audio-visuals and speakers. Preface each category with a covering page describing why that section is there and how it has been designed to further the objectives of the meeting.

The following are some pointers on running the event with your team.

1. Set the rules clearly and simply. Tell everyone what you expect of them and what they can expect from you.

2. Be absolutely clear about who is supposed to do what, and when and where they are supposed to do it.

3. Running a meeting isn't a 9-to-5 job. Be prepared to stay up all night if necessary. Don't give up.

4. Have two fifteen-minute team meetings every day for assigning new priorities, solving problems, and identifying potential problems.

5. Be sensitive to signs of exhaustion and drooping morale. If one of your team is oversensitive, quick to anger, or confused, he or she may need a break and an understanding word.

6. When asking for something, state what it is. For example: "Jim, the stage has to be cleaned up." Then explain why: "Because the game is on next." When it's done, a verbal pat on the back is a priceless morale booster.

7. If there's an argument between team members, defuse it by calmly reminding the participants why they are there. Ask

for their help and thank them for it. "Thanks a lot, guys," you say. "I really appreciate your not getting on each other's nerves here. We'll get this thing done — and we'll do it together."

Now that you have everyone onside and willing to give 101 percent, let's look more closely at the actual logistical situations you are most likely to encounter.

9

LOGISTICS: FOOD, FUN, AND TRANSPORTATION

Food

I've often spoken to people several months after a meeting and found that the only thing they remembered was the food. While food may seem insignificant compared to the message of the meeting, it's not suprising that it so often makes a big impression. Eating, after all, is one of the most direct experiences in life. For many people a meeting is a vacation, a chance to get away from daily routines, including regular diets. They tend to eat more than they do at home. If you want the meeting to be memorable, paying special attention to menus is a sure way to achieve that goal.

Hotel chefs appreciate a chance to be creative. If you're using a Hawaiian or western or seaside motif, for example, work with the chef to design a menu around it, perhaps an elaborate buffet. If the food is all that some of your people will remember a few months later, use it to give them a message about what a class act your organization is and how important it considers its people to be.

Bad food is often more memorable than good food. I remember a banquet where the main course was veal. We were trying to figure out whether it was made of plastic, rubber, or some weird combination of the two. It was simply inedible. So were the buns and the dessert. It could have been a convention of vegetarians because the vegetables were all that anyone ate. That meal cost $3,000 and most of it went into the garbage. How can you prevent such disasters? The following are a few pointers that will help.

1. If you don't know food, if you don't understand how it should be cooked and prepared, delegate responsibility for this important area to someone who does.
2. Remember that different meats have different textures. Veal and chicken are often tough and chewy while fish served to large groups in commercial establishments is often soft and tasteless.
3. Sauces cover a multitude of sins.
4. Marinated meats tend to be softer and easier to eat. Marinated chicken is almost always better than broiled or baked.
5. Pies and quiches are also good bets when serving large groups.
6. Check out the kitchen. What is the predominant method of cooking? How long does food sit in storage before it is cooked and served? It should be less than a day. Where does the hotel get its meat and produce? What is the chef's experience? How much experience has the kitchen had with large meals? You can ask to attend a large banquet behind the scenes, observing the kitchen staff at work and tasting dishes.
7. Go to the establishment and have a meal. If one meal is no good, imagine what two hundred are going to be like.
8. Stick to successful places. Certain hotel chains, for example, Howard Johnson or Holiday Inn, have some of the best meals at some of the best prices. The bigger hotels can afford the best chefs.
9. Be prepared to pay for quality. Those well-known rubber chicken banquets are usually a direct result of penny-pinching. I remember a meeting at a Howard Johnson hotel in which we decided to spend $5 more per person than we had anticipated. That extra $5 resulted in one of the best hotel meals for a large group that I've ever experienced.

Equipment

As the meeting coordinator you're not only managing a large group of people, you're an equipment manager as well. Your technical team may find that it needs some or all of the following: slide, overhead, film, and video projectors; projection screens, including standard, rearview, and front projection screens; staging equipment; tape recorders; amplifiers; speakers;

sound mixers; microphones; cables; fill lights; speaker lights; podiums.

You or the head of your technical team has to decide whether to supply your own equipment or rent equipment. It's best to have your own equipment with you because you're familiar with it and you will have checked it beforehand. But if you're travelling a long distance from home, you'll have to rent equipment on site. Insist on having it delivered at least half a day before the meeting starts so that your technical helpers can make sure everything is working.

Check the telephone book yellow pages under "Audio-Visual Equipment" and "Conference Services" to find the equipment you need. But first check with your hotel to see what equipment it can supply.

In choosing equipment, consider your needs as dictated by your strategy. Do you need audio equipment powerful enough to fill a huge hall? Do you need film or will videotapes do the job?

Keep in mind that all rental equipment has been heavily used. Like a rental car, it needs servicing more often than something carefully used by a single owner. With this in mind, make sure that you can get replacements or repairs quickly, including on weekends and holidays. Never assume that all your equipment is going to work perfectly all of the time. I've never seen it happen.

Talk to your speakers and workshop leaders about the other equipment they will need. This might include flip-charts, chalk-boards, and overheads. (Overheads are overhead projectors that use a large plastic transparency that can be written on; they are useful in seminars and workshops.)

Also in the equipment category is what I call the survival kit (see Figure 9–1). It includes paper clips, rubber bands, tape, glue, hammers, and nails — the little things you're sure to need at some point to deal with equipment, staging, and other problems. This basic list has evolved over my many years of experience in the field of meeting planning. You would be amazed at the number of times that a seemingly insignificant item has saved the day!

Registration

There are three good reasons to run a registration table. The most obvious is security. You might be distributing confidential materials for the eyes of members of your organization only. In

Figure 9–1 Survival Kit List

1. Scissors
2. Packer's knife
3. Stapler and staples
4. Small hammer and nails
5. Carpet tacks
6. Multi-head screwdriver
7. Large and regular paper clips
8. Masking tape
9. Gaffer's tape
10. Cellulose tape
11. Measuring tape (min. 20 ft.)
12. Prepackaged moist towelettes
13. Super-strong glue
14. White glue
15. Chalk
16. Pencils and erasers
17. Pointer
18. Write-on slides
19. Transparencies
20. White-out correction fluid
21. Safety pins
22. Straight pins
23. First-aid kit
24. Sponges
25. Spot remover
26. Needles and thread
27. Mailing labels
28. Blank name tags
29. Loose change (in container)
30. Thumbtacks
31. Push pins
32. Clear nail polish
33. Blank audio cassette
34. Types A, C, and D batteries
35. Extension cord (min. 12 ft.)
36. Phone message pad
37. Small camera and film
38. Throat lozenges
39. Packets of sugar (add a few grains to a glass of water to prevent speakers' dry throat)
40. Stopwatch
41. Box of rubber bands
42. Ball of string
43. Blank $8^1/2$ x 11 sheets of paper
44. Lined pad
45. Small flashlight
46. Nylon cord (min. 50 ft.)
47. Set of felt markers
48. Ballpoint pens
49. Index cards
50. Envelopes (letter size)
51. Empty slide tray (carousel)
52. Small hand brush
53. Compass and protractor set
54. Small plastic container
55. 3-ring binder
56. 3-hole punch
57. Slide holder page
58. Courier envelopes/pouches
59. Hand calculator
60. Metal 15" ruler

that case, it's essential that you identify attendees as they arrive and before they enter the meeting room. The second reason for registering people is to inform them. The registration table is where they can be given the materials and information they need for the meeting. The third reason is acknowledgment. Attendees often get the feeling they're just anonymous members of a crowd. Sitting in the dark watching audio-visuals or in a vast conference room listening to a speaker doesn't give one a strong sense of individuality. That's why it's important to acknowledge that individuality before the meeting begins.

For registrars, you need people with a gift for dealing with people. The more able and experienced these people are, the easier the registration process will be. A good idea, particularly if it's a large meeting and you lack in-house personnel, is to engage off-duty airline flight attendants for this job. These professionals are highly skilled at dealing in an efficient and pleasant manner with large groups of people. You can locate them through airlines or through their unions.

If you have a large gathering it's important to set up your registration desks in a way that enhances, rather than hinders, traffic flow. The individuals must be guided in a pattern of movement that will allow them to get what they need from the registration desk and then get into the meeting, so that there aren't any bottlenecks caused by small groups of people in conversation. The registrars should establish a "safe area" to which individuals with problems and questions can be taken, thus avoiding congestion.

When people haven't seen each other for a year, they want to renew acquaintanceships right away, and they don't worry much about the traffic flow. You should have people on the spot who can politely ask the long-lost friends to step to one side.

Don't clutter your registration desk with materials of only marginal importance. This is the entry to the meeting and the materials distributed must relate strongly to your meeting strategy and key message. Some coordinators make the mistake of just slapping together a pile of "stuff." It's worth the time to design an attractive package that makes a statement, that says to the attendee, "You're special. You're a professional. Here's a kit of material that's of immediate relevance to what you're about to do."

Receptions and Entertainment

Welcoming parties are a good way to set a positive tone for a meeting. Whether alcoholic or not, a party gives people a chance to become acquainted before the meeting starts, to greet old friends, and to meet special guests. The following are some tips on making welcoming parties work.

1. Obtain a room big enough to hold the number of people you invite. Trying to squeeze a hundred people into a hospitality suite more suitable for twenty isn't hospitable.
2. Engage a bartender rather than letting people pour their

own. And ask him or her to go easy and not pour doubles and triples. You don't want a bunch of drunks on your hands.

3. A piano player or a trio of musicians is an elegant touch, but recorded background music is also pleasant.

4. If you want to be sure that people mingle, arrange the seating so that small groups can't sequester themselves off in the corners.

Often an organization's suppliers are happy to sponsor a hospitality suite during a meeting. Liquor companies sometimes will do the same.

Entertainment usually is presented in the evenings. The meeting's over and everyone goes out to a show or a ball game. There's nothing wrong with that but there's also nothing wrong with entertainment being presented at other times of day. I like to schedule some entertainment in the afternoon, followed by more work sessions in the early evening. The entertainment breaks up the day, generates a lot of energy, and leaves people invigorated for the work that follows.

I ran a meeting for a manufacturing company on the theme, "One Step into the Future." On the second afternoon, we took everyone to a futuristic display featuring a "space ride." Afterward people had plenty of energy to resume the work part of the meeting with a discussion about changes to come in manufacturing, which tied right in with the entertainment.

Tying entertainment into your strategy isn't hard. If your theme is competition, then a sports event can tie in well and can be used to illustrate some important point such as, in Yogi Berra's immortal words, "It ain't over 'til it's over." An evening on a large sailboat would be a clever way to illustrate a theme such as "Steer Your Own Course" or "Take Over the Wheel in Your Sales Territory."

But don't feel compelled to link your entertainment to your theme. In fact, entertainment is the one area of your program where you can safely stray from your central strategy. I ran a meeting on the theme of improving competitiveness by becoming more professional. Our entertainment was a Chinese acrobatic group. They were professionals, it's true, but that wasn't the point. The reason for booking them was that the show was a total break from what people had been thinking about during the day and it recharged them for the next day's work. When you're planning to book entertainment acts, one of the best places to start is in the yellow pages of your phone book under "Entertainment" or "Party entertainment." You can also check the entertainment section of your local newspaper and contact interesting acts directly through the clubs or theaters at which they are appearing.

Talent agencies and professional theater groups are other sources of talent. There are some top-notch professionals who specialize in performing at business meetings. A notable example is the comedian Ray Baumel. If you haven't heard of him, that makes him happy because anonymity is an important part of his act.

Baumel's favorite character is Dr. Marcellino Gonzalez who, in a thick Spanish accent, addresses meetings of some of the largest corporations in the world. If he's addressing Gulf Oil, he's an expert on the oil industry. He mingles with the audience before the speech, boring them with pedantic comments.

The opening minutes of his speech are both credible and sleep-inducing. The audience thinks it's hearing yet another knowledgeable but dull expert. It has no idea what's in store. Suddenly, Gonzalez begins to jabber incoherently and the dozing audience perks up, wondering if the guest speaker is having a nervous breakdown.

At that moment, perhaps, he'll turn on the company's treasurer, sitting at the head table, and compliment him for being "a fine man, shy and retiring. He's shy about $12,000. That's why he's retiring." Then he'll glare at the chairman of the board: "I've heard a lot about you. Someday I'm going to hear your side." By this time, the audience is in hysterics.

Talent like that doesn't come cheap and Ray Baumel collects $5,000 per appearance. Of course, there are good acts for less than that. But don't expect to put a show on for nothing and get good results. One of my most painful memories is of a husband-and-wife team of entertainers that was selected by the president of a company. Many people walked out on them and some fell asleep. It was embarrassing.

You have to be careful in choosing your entertainment, as one coordinator learned the hard way. His company had operations in South Africa but nevertheless liked to claim that its ethics were among the highest. In fact, ethics was a theme of the meeting. The planner had the bright idea of taking people to see a play by a black South African playwright. Unfortunately for him, he didn't know that his own company's hiring practices were lambasted in the play. That evening wasn't one of the meeting's high points.

If the coordinator had checked out the play beforehand, he could have avoided embarrassment. Always talk to the individuals you intend to book and try to see them in performance. If that's not possible, ask to see a videotape. Don't trust blind luck because it rarely works.

A final point on the subject of entertainment is that there's nothing wrong with doing nothing. Some coordinators play social director and try to fill every waking minute with some mental or physical activity. That can be exhausting. People need time to be by themselves, go for a walk, or sit in the sun. Don't forget to leave some "do-nothing" time in your schedule.

Special Needs

A meeting coordinator's life is not a simple one. People are individuals and your attendees will have many special interests and special needs. One is dietary. Perhaps some people need diabetic, kosher, or vegetarian meals. It's an insult to someone if he or she hasn't been respected enough to have these needs determined in advance. It's easy enough to do. During the teaser or pre-meeting campaign, send out a questionnaire asking people if they have any special dietary or health-related needs. This makes a good impression even on the majority who have no such needs. They will think, "I'm not just a number to this organization. I matter." What about your attendees' spouses or companions? They aren't going to be an integral part of the meeting but they shouldn't be ignored. There are people who specialize in companion programs and they can be located through such meeting organizations as Meeting Planners International or in the yellow pages under "Conference Services."

My advice is not to try to set up your own companions' program. This is definitely one area in which most of us need an outside consultant's help. If, however, you do go ahead on your own, the following are some key rules to keep in mind.

1. Send out a questionnaire during the pre-meeting campaign that asks the companions of the attendees what they might like to see. People often have firm ideas about what they would like to do.

2. Put your transportation requirements in the hands of a professional transportation company, bus line, or tour line. You don't want the companions sweltering on some dingy yellow school bus on a hot July day.
3. Take care of the little needs such as refreshment stops and washroom breaks.
4. Look for unusual things to do rather than, or in addition to, the standard fashion show and museum visit. Perhaps there's a science center with a hands-on display. Or a big Chinatown full of exotic shops. Maybe the annual crafts fair coincides with your meeting. One of our most popular companion events was an afternoon with palm readers, crystal-ball gazers, and horoscope makers. Check out the entertainment sections of the newspapers and ask the local tourist bureau for a list of upcoming events.
5. Make sure that each participant gets a kit of materials that includes maps and brochures about the places they will be visiting.

Language differences present yet another problem. If you have guests coming from Japan or Quebec or Mexico, don't assume that they speak English. Find out beforehand if interpreters are required.

If you have foreign guests or government representatives, there are protocol problems to be considered. It's easy to insult someone. I was involved in a meeting that required a display of flags from the homelands of the various guests. A flag manufacturer produced the flags for us and managed to put the bars in the wrong direction on the South Korean flag. As a result, we had to mollify some miffed Koreans.

How do you address a cabinet minister or an ambassador or a religious dignitary? These aren't trivial matters, particularly if the people are invited guests. Governments — federal, provincial and state, and local — have experts in protocol and a few calls will get you the answers you need.

Disaster Protection

The final logistical problem is disaster protection, mainly against sickness and fire. Hotels and other meeting sites have doctors on call. Find out who the doctors are and place a clause in your hotel letter of agreement that one will be available at all times during the meeting. Know where the closest hospitals are and how to locate an emergency dentist.

The National Insurance Association and the Insurance Bureau of Canada have films on fires in hotels and what to do about them. These are available free of charge and I recommend showing one of them to the attendees at the beginning of the meeting. You should also run a fire drill. Some might call this an unnecessary precaution. However, you have hundreds of people on your hands and if they panic, even during a small fire, the result could be injury or even death.

Check with the hotel about what liability insurance it carries. If it's not adequate, check with your own agents and arrange for more coverage. Liability settlements can run into the millions of dollars. As a meeting planner, I personally carry $1 million in liability coverage. That means if something falls on someone's head and I am sued, I am covered for $1 million. If you're not covered and the hotel or conference center lacks sufficient coverage, then you or your company or organization are in a precarious position. Why take unneccessary chances?

Transportation

Transportation is part of your meeting. An individual's meeting experience starts the moment he or she enters the plane, train, or bus. You can't control what happens on the plane but you can do your best to make sure the travel arrangements are in order. The easiest and best way to do this is to find a reliable, knowledgeable travel agency and let it take care of the bookings. Some organizations prefer to make travel arrangements in-house, believing they have better control that way. But it doesn't cost anything to use an agent and in some cases it's even cheaper. In addition to regular travel agents, there are people who specialize in ground transportation, including some meeting planners who are experts in this field. The logistics of getting a few hundred people into a vehicle or series of vehicles and having them arrive on time with all their baggage are complicated. So why not leave that headache to the professionals?

You can begin to exercise control the moment your guests enter the air terminal or train station. Reception is a significant part of transportation. A warm reception from the host at the airport is an excellent way to communicate to your guests the way you feel about them and their contribution to your organization.

Once I handled a meeting but I wasn't given responsibility for the reception. I wound up being jealous of the people who did handle it because they did such a fine job. When the attendees arrived at the airport, they were greeted by charming creatures, people in costumes representing the seven dwarfs from *Snow White*. Each dwarf had a rickshaw and pulled two people at a time out of the terminal to the limousine that would take them to the hotel. The guests were surprised and delighted and it was a wonderful start to the meeting.

On one occasion, I set up at the airport a booth that looked like Lucy's psychiatrist booth in the "Peanuts" comic strip. In the booth was a man dressed in a doctor's white coat. He analyzed the "patients" one by one and gave each a "prescription." When they arrived at the hotel, they handed the prescription in at another booth to get their room key and a gift. This welcome tied in with our theme, which was that the company, a battery manufacturer, had been through some tough times but that some "good medicine" had succeeded in curing most of the problems. Humor is one of the nicest ways to impart a message.

Accommodations

Many hotels boast that they possess superb meeting facilities on excellent sites. But you have to see it to believe it. My experience is that renting a facility sight unseen is a recipe for nasty surprises — ratty carpets, burned-out lights, and slide projectors that don't function. Even if you saw the hotel last year, it's advisable to check it out again. Hotels deteriorate quickly. Three years of ordinary use can turn a brand-new hotel into a shambles if management fails to invest sufficiently in upkeep.

As well as inspecting the hotel, you must also inspect the locale. A hotel doesn't just float in the air by itself. Two Holiday Inns might be identical in construction but if one is on the beach at Boca Raton, Florida, and the other is in downtown Newark, they are two quite different hotels.

Depending on your strategy, the Newark site might well be the better choice. The planning team might want a purely business environment because business is more important than relaxation at that particular moment in your organization's history. It might plan on bringing a lot of senior people in from New York, Toronto, or Chicago to speak to the meeting and a site like Newark would be more accessible than Florida.

Or perhaps it's part of the strategy to impress people with the grandeur and professionalism of the organization. A five-star, grand hotel in the heart of the city might be a necessity in such circumstances. On the other hand, if developing a sense of family in the organization is part of what the strategists want to achieve, then you probably need a smaller, quieter property.

Perhaps you want to give your people a chance to find out something new about themselves. You might want them to do some long-term thinking about the organization's future in a relaxed and informal environment. They won't be able to do this in a busy downtown site. Your strategy, therefore, would dictate the choice of a resort hotel.

THE LETTER OF AGREEMENT

The letter of agreement that you will sign with the hotel is an important document. The letter of agreement itemizes everything that the hotel will do for you. I have put together letters of agreement that contained as many as seven hundred separate items. To understand the importance of a letter of agreement, you have to understand the economics of the hotel industry.

Hotels sell three things — rooms, food, and beverages, preferably alcoholic. Selling those three things is how they make most of their money. Food and alcoholic beverages are high-margin items and the hotel wants to sell as much of those as it possibly can. Everything else — including meeting facilities — is peripheral. They are there as a means of drawing customers who will eat, drink, and sleep in the hotel.

Therefore, the hotel manager's chief concern is filling rooms, restaurants, and bars. To the extent that meeting facilities can achieve this, they are important but they aren't the first priority. They are *your* first priority, however, and the letter of agreement is the weapon you need to make sure that you get what you are paying for. It makes things easier for both you and the hotel.

When you visit the site, take copious notes about everything you see. Back in your office, think about everything you will need for what you want to accomplish. For instance, you might need special breakout rooms that are separate from your main meeting room where you can hold small conferences, panel discussions, or workshops. If you're running a master workshop on product analysis and you want to break the attendees out into groups of five, you will need five breakout rooms near the central meeting area. You might also need special equipment and the assistance of hotel staff.

Once I was amazed to discover staff at a hotel tearing down some elaborate stages that we had set up the night before a meeting. When I asked why, I was told the room had to be cleared for "another meeting." I stopped the destruction and got the manager on the phone. There had been a mix-up and the staff was trying to make way for the meeting we had already set up for. Even though they had been properly informed, they had misunderstood. This incident is a good illustration of the importance of having all of your arrangements with the hotel in writing.

Ask about fire regulations. What are they and are they available in printed form? Is there a film available on what to do in case of fire. What does the hotel do in case of fire? There have been several tragic hotel fires in recent years, including the horrific disasters in Las Vegas and Puerto Rico. There's no longer the slightest excuse, if ever there was one, for not being conscious of the danger and taking preventative steps.

Ask about lights and electrical outlets. Are the rooms bright enough? Are the chandeliers big enough? Are they high enough so that your displays are all well illuminated?

Can you put decorations up on the ceilings and pin notices to the walls? Does the hotel have restrictions on where you can put up direction signs?

How is the seating in the banquet room? Are there too many pillars blocking the view of the stage? Will you be able to fit in all the chairs and tables you want, arranged as you want?

Are photocopying and facsimile machines, typewriters, and other office supplies available? Are they available on the weekend? If you need to install a bank of computers as part of your program, will that present any problems to the hotel?

Are there telephones in the meeting room that you can use while you're setting up and during the meeting? Is there any danger that those phones will ring in the middle of an important speech, disturbing everyone in the room? (That's happened to me.)

If yours is an international association or a company with foreign branches, you might require simultaneous translation for parts of your program. Ask if the hotel has had any experience in setting up booths for simultaneous translation.

How accessible is the hotel to major highways, to the airport, to the subway system? Are there oversized doors for the car or large pieces of machinery that you want to display?

Does the hotel have lots of bedrooms but only one meeting room? Or does it have plenty of meeting rooms but a shortage of bedrooms?

Are extra waiters and other service people you might need for special events easily available and well trained? What about such personal services as beauty salons, barbers, and dry cleaners? Are pets allowed?

Sometimes the hotel's power supply isn't sufficient for all of the lighting you want and all the equipment you plan to run. Can generators be brought in or can you bring in extra power directly from electricity lines?

If you want to have a welcome gift in everybody's room, will the hotel put them there and how much, if anything, will it charge for doing so?

Are there quick check-out facilities? Is there adequate parking for buses and limos? Are there special suites and special treatment for distinguished guest speakers?

What are noise levels in the hotel like? What is the traffic flow like? Will it take someone twenty minutes to get from his or her room on the nineteenth floor of the tower to the conference room?

What about confidentiality? You may be discussing confidential information that you wouldn't want a competitor or the press to have. Are you sure no one can sneak in through one of the service doors and listen to the proceedings?

Before you strike any deal with the hotel, write all of your needs down in simple, numbered sentences. For example:

1. We need the time of three members of the hotel staff for three days, eight hours a day.
2. We need a round table to seat sixteen people.
3. We need two screens, 8 feet by 40 feet (2.5 m x 12 m).

and so on. On receiving the letter, the manager will let you know what he or she can or can't do and will quote you a price.

Striking a deal with the hotel isn't as simple as buying a car. In some cases, the room rates will include the extra labor you will need from the hotel's staff. Your letter of agreement may include several hundred items. What is the hotel prepared to give you?

What is going to cost extra? Remember that what you get for the price you're paying is a more important issue than the price itself.

A good hotel will not quote you a vastly inflated price in the hope that you'll be dumb enough to pay it. The business is competitive and the hotel knows that a customer who feels ripped-off won't come back and will tell many others why. So how much negotiating space do you have? That varies, but it's usually between fifteen and twenty percent. Much depends on the size of your meeting. If you're spending $500,000, you've obviously got lots of leverage.

As a buyer of a large quantity of rooms, you can expect some discount from what an individual hotel guest would pay. The amount depends on the type of hotel, the season, and the location. It might vary from five percent in a luxury hotel to as much as twenty percent in a lower-priced establishment. If you are booking a meeting between December 10 and January 10, you may be able to bargain a discount of up to thirty percent because many city hotels are largely empty during that period. Other hotels, however, won't even do that.

Don't expect discounts on food and beverages. The hard fact of life is that hotels make most of their money selling bedrooms, food, and drink. Renting out meeting rooms doesn't do much for their bottom line and you can bet they will want to recoup on the refreshments. That means the cup of coffee that costs 75 cents in the hotel coffee shop will cost you $1 when it's wheeled into the meeting area.

Your total cost will depend on such variables as where your meeting is held, the class of hotel, and the number of people to be accommodated. Currently, a three-day meeting for one hundred people in a good downtown hotel in a major North American city should cost between $500 and $1,000 per person, including transportation. If you're starting fresh, get quotes from three different potential sites. But if you've had previous meetings and been satisfied, and have assured yourself that the hotel is maintaining its standards, why switch? Too often, bargain hunters end up with a shabby meeting site when they already knew about a good one.

There are a couple of danger signs to watch for when negotiating for accommodation. If the hotel suddenly changes salespeople on you, bringing in the sales director or someone else with more clout and more aggressiveness, it means that the hotel's management is trying hard to close a deal. Don't sign unless you're certain it's a good deal.

If the salesperson insists that you sign immediately, even though the meeting is seven or eight months away, I suggest you back off. Seven months isn't necessarily out of line these days for reserving meeting facilities. However, if you feel you're getting the high-pressure treatment, it won't hurt to wait a few days, check out the competition, and get some perspective on matters.

DIPLOMACY PAYS OFF

Don't ignore the hotel staff and don't treat them as if they were part of the furniture. If you treat them well and acknowledge their help, they will give you the service you need.

I ran a meeting for a packaged-goods company that was introducing a new fruit-based product. The vice president of marketing was a very smart man who proved that smart people can do stupid things. He went to the banquet staff and insisted that they serve samples of the new product in the meeting room. This was news to them and when they seemed reluctant, he insisted, pointing out that "Even an idiot could do this, so why don't you guys just listen to me and do what you're told?"

Just before the point in the meeting at which the samples were to be served, all of the servers mysteriously disappeared. The vice president, in a panic, told me to find them and deal with the problem. I located the banquet manager and managed to collect ten of the banquet staff. I apologized for the way they had been spoken to and explained that we really needed their help and could they please lend a hand. They did and each one received an envelope later containing $5 and a thank-you note. It cost $50 to resolve a bad situation that would never had arisen had the vice president of marketing exerted a little common courtesy. I charged the $50 to him.

It's best to get off on the right foot with the hotel staff. I like to call them together before the meeting begins. I tell them what the meeting is about, what we will expect of them, and I refer to the letter of agreement. I also give them small gifts — for instance, discount coupons for a fast-food restaurant. It doesn't cost much to get the staff on your side and it's a wise investment. When the event is over, if it went well and you might use the same site again, send the manager and staff a thank-you letter. They'll be behind you one hundred percent the next time.

ALTERNATIVE ACCOMMODATIONS

Hotels, of course, are not the only possible sites for holding meetings. University campuses, convention centers, and conference centers in rural settings are all in the business of renting meeting facilities. Many of their customers are non-profit or academic organizations on a tight budget. The advantage for you is that, unlike a hotel, these places have no large mortgage and numerous staff members to pay; you reap the reward in the form of lower prices.

The disadvantage is that you get less. These non-hotel sites often are less well-equipped to handle such issues as noise and confidentiality. A convention center I used lacked walls to limit noise. That was a serious problem, with two meetings going on at the same time. They're also not as flexible as a hotel. Coffee is at 11 a.m. and not 11:30. Your meeting had better stop at 10 p.m. because their staff can't wait around until 10:30. They often do not have the facilities to handle audio-visual and other equipment.

In general, you can get better service out of a smaller, less expensive hotel than you will get at any of these alternate sites. Use them only if budget is a prime consideration.

Traffic Control Planning

In checking out a meeting site, imagine what it's going to look like with a hundred or a thousand people in it. Too many people in a small room is a crowd. Put the same number in a big room and it looks like nobody came. Consider such things as the availability of washrooms and phones. If, for example, the phones are too far away, every coffee break is going to be prolonged as a result and you'll have to adjust your schedule accordingly.

Your traffic control planning starts even before you visit the site, and includes the following steps.

1. Order a plan of the hotel or conference center. Determine where the meeting rooms are located relative to each other and to the front desk. Note the locations of elevators, washrooms, phones, and fire exits, and where the hallways and stairs are located relative to the meeting rooms. Now you're prepared for the on-site examination.

2. Walk through the site as follows:
   - start at the front door and walk to the meeting room
   - go from the meeting room to a guest room
   - go from the elevators to the meeting room
   - go from the elevators to the phones to the washrooms
   - go from the meeting rooms to the fire exits to the hall-ways to the stairs
   - go from the fire exits, hallways, and stairs to the elevators
   - go from the meeting rooms and the guest rooms to the front lobby, the patios in front of the building, and the parking lots.

3. Analyze what you've learned from your walkabout. You need to know how many steps each of these trips takes. Each trip should be no longer than about one hundred steps or take longer than two minutes. I have been in hotels in which it takes eight minutes to go from one area to another. Usually, these are properties to which conference centers have been added after the main construction was completed. These sites have problems. People can get tired out walking from one area to another. They can get lost. They can meet people and get distracted. They start out planning to do one thing and wind up doing another. If you're trying to move a hundred people from Point A to Point B in such an environment, you're almost guaranteed to suffer some attrition.

4. During your walk, look for areas of congestion such as narrow hallways, or two elevators where there should be three, or an area that's busy with non-meeting traffic. You should check these areas at three different times of day — 8 to 9 a.m., noon, and about 4 p.m. These are the times when hotel traffic is busiest and if you do a walkabout during those times you will be able to figure out what things will be like during your meeting. Suppose you are going to have one hundred people at your meeting. If you've taken 90 steps to get from one place to another and it took you 1.5 minutes, you can multiply that by a factor of 5. You now know that it will take 7.5 minutes to move all one hundred people from Point A to Point B. This type of information is essential in planning your agenda. If the refreshment area is one hundred steps from the meeting area, you know it is going to be about thirty minutes from the beginning of the break to the resumption of the meeting.

10

AFTER THE BALL IS OVER

Every meeting has its critics. There are always people who think they know better than the meeting planners who should have been invited to speak, what items should have been discussed, and how the meeting in general should have been handled. This kind of "I-told-you-so" criticism is unconstructive, but that doesn't mean a "postmortem" shouldn't be held. On the contrary, a postmortem should follow every meeting to identify the positive elements in hopes of repeating them with greater frequency the next year. Each meeting should be seen as a chance to get better rather than as an opportunity to look for new mistakes.

The hands-on coordinator is the person closest to the meeting. Although not responsible for the original design objectives, the coordinator fully understands them and is, therefore, the best person to take charge of the postmortem. The senior executive should then analyze the results, looking for factors that might affect future meetings.

Not finding any mistakes is not necessarily good news. I did a meeting for a large client in the information-systems business. The meeting was attended by almost a thousand people at a cost of $580,000. It was a one-day event and, for the first time in my experience, it was flawless. Nobody could find a single thing that went wrong.

But when I sat down with the client for the postmortem, we agreed that although the meeting was perfect in its execution, it wasn't a success. It didn't reach its objective, which had been to make the sales force feel positive about the extensive changes that had taken place in the company. Admittedly, there had been too much change too fast. The point we wanted to make was that these changes were now over and that they were beneficial. But the attendees wouldn't accept that because they lacked confidence in management.

In analyzing our failure, we decided that the fault lay partly in areas over which we had had no control and partly in areas that we did. There was nothing recriminatory in any of the discussion because we really were talking about what we should do the next time. I delivered a series of recommendations for improving the next year's event that coincided with the client's own thinking. Thus the postmortem served as a positive move forward into the next meeting.

Mistakes are only bad if they lead absolutely nowhere. They can be used to your advantage if you see them as indicators of where you can do better next time. Improvement in meeting planning comes from a process of elimination and from learning and doing. That's why a postmortem can be so helpful. You can use it to eliminate those things that didn't work, or should have been done differently, or didn't produce quite the effects you wanted.

What most often happens in postmortems is that the planners say, "I think we achieved what we wanted to do." That's not good enough. The answer should be, "Yes, we had definite indications that we achieved the attitude change or skills improvement or increased motivation that we wanted. We know that because we've measured it against definite standards."

The postmortem should analyze where the meeting deviated from what had been predicted. In planning a meeting you should always expect a certain amount of deviation. No plan is perfect. Perhaps you thought an audio-visual would have a certain effect and it turned out to have the opposite effect, and a negative one at that. Or perhaps it had an unexpected, but positive, impact.

Analyzing these deviations is tremendously helpful for your future planning. It strengthens your ability to prevent unwanted deviations from occurring. And it allows you to insert positive elements deliberately rather than leaving them to chance.

Handling the Meeting Postmortem

1. Collect all your written records of the meeting. These include your notes and those taken by members of your team and any other written records. If someone made videos of parts of the meeting, get those as well.
2. Ask each key team member responsible for such areas as

travel, entertainment, audio-visuals, and food to prepare a one-page report of how the meeting went from his or her perspective.

3. Get in touch with all suppliers of goods and services such as the hotel, the audio-visual producer, and any consultants you might have used. Ask their opinion on how the meeting went and don't take "Fine" for an answer. There must have been one or two problems. Remember, you're not looking for reasons to accuse anybody. You just want to find ways to improve next year's meeting.

4. Bring all the key team members and planners together for one meeting. Review the record and get everyone's overall impressions, paying special attention to any outstanding successes. Then the problems are discussed and the lessons that have been drawn from those problems. Each person should make recommendations on how things could be improved next year. Out of this meeting comes an action plan outlining all the recommendations for improving things, who will be responsible for executing those recommendations, and when.

5. Collect each team member's report, the action plan, and any other relevant information in one complete postmortem report. Keep a copy on file and circulate copies to all your key people.

6. If someone else will be organizing the meeting next year, prepare an executive summary for that person. In one hundred words or less, tell that person exactly what happened this year and what to watch out for next year. That will give the new person a quick grasp of the situation before he or she delves into the full report.

I remember doing a postmortem with one client after the first meeting I had run for him. We discovered certain areas where we felt new elements were needed next time. The salespeople attending the meeting needed help with their performance in the field but they didn't want someone preaching at them. At the next meeting, we decided to hold a business game in which a host spins a wheel that selects topics. He or she then takes questions out of envelopes and asks members of the audience for the answers.

In our meeting, the questions related to the company and its products and history. Some if it was pretty trivial but it got people involved, talking among themselves, and feeling good about the company.

Although we had expected good things from the business game, it was twice as successful as we had hoped. We had hoped that about twenty-five of the sixty people attending would participate; as it happened only five declined to participate.

In our postmortem, we decided to expand on that success. In the third year, therefore, we added an additional business game. And it was still more successful because people looked forward to it and came in mentally prepared.

Had we not sat down and systematically analyzed the positive effects of that first business game we would not have been in a position to extract as much benefit from it as we did in subsequent years. Six months later we would have been wondering what to try this year.

Avoiding Postmortem Avoidance

The benefits of doing a proper postmortem are obvious, and it's a simple process. So why isn't it done more often? One reason is based on my greatest complaint about most meeting planners: they have a logistical rather than a goal orientation to meetings. The mechanics are what interest them. "Let's get the darned thing done and done right," they say, "and we'll worry about everything else later." They would get better results if instead they said, "Let's achieve what we set out to do and let's analyze it afterward to make sure that we did achieve it. If we didn't, let's find out why. If we did, let's make sure we can do it again."

It's perfectly natural once a large meeting is concluded for the coordinator to breathe a huge sigh of relief and turn his or her attention to other things. "That's done with and I don't have to worry about it again until next year," is the attitude.

Worry is the operative word here because worrying is exactly what that coordinator will be doing three months before the next meeting. Ironically, if only a thorough postmortem were done after the meeting, there would be so much less to worry about because he or she would have a clear idea of how to handle the next meeting. He or she would feel in control. It's unfortunate that so many people see a meeting as a big headache to be suffered through and forgotten until the next one.

Yet another reason for avoiding postmortems is the fear of bad news. Some people don't *want* to know what went wrong. They don't want to talk about it. There was a problem? Forget it. Next year is another year.

Yet another reason is the concept of meetings as one-time projects rather than as part of a continuing program. Often the coordinator accepts the task on the understanding that it is for one time only and the job is to be passed on to someone else the next year. In that situation, the organizer has no motivation to do a postmortem.

Even people who run the same organization's meeting every year often take the attitude that it's a one-time project. The meeting is viewed as an annual problem to be handled and then forgotten.

The program approach realizes that meetings are part of an evolutionary process and that they do not happen in isolation. The business year and the marketing year and the operations year of a company develop in a certain way. So should the internal communications year. Companies are always analyzing their marketing to see how it can be improved. Why not take the same approach to internal communications?

Meeting Postmortem Tools

QUESTIONNAIRES

Your first tool in doing a postmortem is the questionnaire (see Figure 10-1). You want to hear from your audience whether you achieved what you set out to do and whether any significant change occurred. Questionnaires should be written to elicit feelings more than facts, because facts can be deceptive. A person may answer that yes, she attended all of the sessions and yes, she understood all of the information. But that doesn't tell you enough. She might still have a negative attitude toward what she learned.

Ask your attendees whether they were satisfied with the meeting. Ask what turned turned them on and what turned them off. Ask them whether their overall assessment was negative or positive and why.

In the seemingly perfect meeting I referred to above, some of the audience was so hung over from partying the night before that they were almost asleep. This was evident not only from their blurry-eyed condition but also from their responses later to the questionnaire, in which most of them indicated a preference for starting the sessions later in the day.

Figure 10–1 Postmortem Questionnaire

Seminar Analysis

Please answer the questions below by placing a check (✔) in the appropriate box. Additional space has been left for comments you'd like to make:

1. Did the seminar address the
   issues you wanted?

Yes	Mostly	Not Sure	A Bit	No

2. Was the information given in an
   easy to understand way?

Yes	Mostly	Not Sure	A Bit	No

3. Was the presenter informative
   and entertaining?

Yes	Mostly	Not Sure	A Bit	No

4. Did you have enough chance
   to participate?

Yes	Mostly	Not Sure	A Bit	No

5. Did you get a clear idea of how
   to apply what you learned?

Yes	Mostly	Not Sure	A Bit	No

6. Were there enough opportunities
   for questions?

Yes	Mostly	Not Sure	A Bit	No

7. Are there any other comments
   you'd like to add?

Yes	Mostly	Not Sure	A Bit	No

It wasn't until lunch time that they began to wake up. In responding to the questionnaire, they also indicated that the very flawlessness of the meeting's logistics was off-putting. They felt it was too polished and lacked the personal touch.

We had tried to put a message across via a slick, professional theatrical performance. In the postmortem, we decided that we would have been better off using a heavy-metal rock band. The audience was young and aggressive and that sort of music would have energized them at the morning session. The band should have been followed by a highly motivational speaker who would appeal to their emotions rather than to their intellects. The speaker we used gave a logical and thoughtful presentation, but he wasn't in tune with the audience.

Our analysis also showed that the meeting was beyond the understanding of the attendees. They did not grasp the message because some fundamental issues were glossed over. These issues concerned both internal politics and the company's external relations with governmental regulatory bodies. Without some understanding of these issues, it was impossible to make sense of the organizational changes that were taking place in the company.

All of this gave us a good idea of how to go about things next time. We now knew to change the agenda so that people wouldn't be hung over for the important sessions. We would do this by arranging for them to arrive in the morning and start the meeting after lunch, before they had a chance to party. Instead they could network, relax, and generally acclimatize themselves before getting down to business.

We also knew that we had to work more motivation into the meeting. Without a questionnaire that probed the respondents' feelings, we might have obtained a lot of standard responses and not realized the truth.

Questionnaires must be distributed within two to six weeks after the event. My own practice is never to wait longer than two weeks. The longer you wait, the less accurate a response you're likely to get. What you need are accurate feelings and specific facts. What you'll get after six weeks are generalities.

A questionnaire format that is short and easy to answer is the Likert Scale. It's a five-point continuum that goes from "yes" to "no" with "not sure" right in the middle (refer back to Figure 10.1). You can assign numbers to the points along the continuum so that you can total the responses and come up with actual percentages. You need to poll at least ten percent of the audience to get a valid response; anything less might be reflective of one particular group.

In addition to multiple-choice questions, you should ask questions that require essay-type answers, which allow people the opportunity to express themselves fully. Some sample questions might be: What was your overall feeling about the meeting? Explain in detail. What changes would you make if you were in charge of the meeting and could do it all over again? Which part of the meeting did you like the most? Which did you like the least?

INTERVIEWS

Sometimes the answers to a questionnaire produce new questions. As a result, you might want to follow up by personally interviewing a cross section of the attendees. Obviously, the larger your sample, the more representative it will be. However, a ten percent sample usually is enough to give you an accurate picture.

I organized a meeting for a cookie manufacturing company and followed up with a postmortem questionnaire. The response was highly enthusiastic, so much so that we decided to probe more deeply to find out why.

What we found was something quite simple: the attendees liked the meeting because they were starved for communication. "We should have a meeting like that every month," was a frequent suggestion. But the company didn't need to spend $100,000 a month on a meeting for all its employees. We were able to set up a follow-up program to increase internal communications through newsletters and other means at a modest cost. That internal communications program probably never would have been established had not our post-meeting interviews pinpointed the need so dramatically.

Your postmortem should also include a financial analysis. You might find, for example, that the level of spending increased as the meeting progressed. That could have been caused by flaws in the original design that required costly on-the-spot correction. For instance, you might have failed to allow enough time to demonstrate a new product and had to scramble at the last minute to arrange additional demonstrations and additional supporting materials, which all cost extra. The financial analysis can tell you a lot about how effective your early planning was.

Correcting those design flaws will save you money the next time.

Examine the usefuless of materials distributed during the meeting. If that three-ring binder that cost you $100 is gathering dust on a shelf, it means that you failed to get people sufficiently involved with the special materials inside. These things should be used again almost immediately after the meeting when the attendees' enthusiasm is still high. For example, information learned in a workshop on sales techniques can be put to use immediately in the field. If the workbook isn't being used, something is wrong. Too often, organizers blithely say, "Oh, I'm sure they're using it." The fact is that you can't be sure they're using it unless you ask.

I ran a product-knowledge seminar for salesmen of a consumer goods company. After the meeting, sales of the product doubled. Through anecdotal reports from the salesmen themselves, we were able to establish a causal relationship between the seminar and the increased sales. In interviews with the attendees, we also discovered that those who were not reporting increases were those who didn't have a good grasp of the subject matter of the seminars. That was a straightforward way of measuring results based on empirical evidence.

It seems so simple, yet too often it's not done. A company runs a meeting to introduce a new product and then makes no attempt to relate subsequent sales to the effects of the meeting. Now of course, a cause-and-effect relationship isn't always as easy to establish as it was in the above case. But that doesn't mean you shouldn't try to find out if what was learned at the meeting is paying off in the field.

The views of your organization's executives also are important. Find out why they did or did not like the meeting. Perhaps they objected to something about the style of the event. There may be a way to design the next one in a fashion that better reflects the philosophy of the key people in the organization while still catering effectively to your audience.

The Final Analysis

A crucial part of the postmortem is the analysis of the notes that the meeting coordinator made while the event was in progress. For this purpose, I usually carry a bright-red pen along with my flowcharts, in a binder. The notes I take during the meeting are answers to such questions as: Did that element go well? Was it on time? How could it have been changed? What was the problem? Where was the problem? If enough time wasn't allowed for a certain aspect of the meeting, plans should be made now to correct it next time. Why go through all the same mistakes and hassles a second time?

The exact points on the flowchart where problems occurred should be isolated. If there were only two problems out of one hundred elements, that's not necessarily good news, particularly if those two were critical and their failure meant that the entire meeting design ended up in a mess. Getting ninety-eight out of one hundred things right won't be much consolation if a mismanaged travel schedule ruins the carefully planned opening of your meeting because only half of the attendees arrived on time. The pain will be even greater if the second of the two problems was a technical flaw with a complicated product display that caused a delay, resulting in the cancellation of a crucial workshop because the hotel had already promised the room to another group.

In red ink, the meeting coordinator should note how many problems occurred in each section of the meeting. How many audio-visual problems were there? Were there difficulties involving the guest speakers? If you know which were the problems areas, special attention can be paid to them next time.

Analyze the Murphy's Law Antidote list. How accurate were the predictions of what might go wrong and how useful were the preventive and remedial measures? If a problem did occur despite the preventive measures, obviously they weren't good enough and a better way will have to be found. If the remedy didn't work well either, that's two failures and it's time to analyze the situation even more closely.

During one meeting, I needed printed information from which to create slides to provide the audio-visual support for a speaker. As a student of Murphy's Law, I had predicted that the client would be late in providing the information. As a preventive measure, I had special forms made up with dates on them, showing when overtime charges would be imposed by the audio-visual firm. I figured that showing the client how much being late would cost would get him moving.

I had also planned a remedial measure. If looming overtime charges failed to extract the necessary information, I would insist on getting the information verbally rather than waiting for the client to send it in. The prevention failed because the client was willing to pay the overtime and the remedy failed because the client refused to see me, saying he was too busy.

The result was that the slides had to be made at the very last minute, at a cost of $9,000 more than had been projected. In the postmortem, I explained to the client how my attempts to avoid the cost overrun had failed and suggested that he should find a way to avoid such a thing in the future.

We've now developed a system whereby the client provides raw information, we analyze it and put it into slides that the client then approves. The client does less work, pays less money, and is happy. I do more work. It's the kind of good thing that can happen when you take postmortems seriously.

What this incident demonstrates is that the root cause of a problem is always a person. You can't blame problems on machines or on schedules because someone had the job of making sure that the machine worked and someone devised that schedule.

At the end, the coordinator should try to put the postmortem into perspective. The meeting should be analyzed as part of something larger, as part of the ongoing growth and development of your organization. Failing to do this can lead to exaggerating either the success or the failure of the meeting. Don't let your staff be mesmerized by the great job that they did; they might go into the next meeting feeling cocky and mess it up. Putting it all into perspective allows everyone to make intelligent decisions to follow up the meeting just finished and prepare for the next one.

Go back to the fundamentals. Why was the meeting held? Was that the right reason? Were the objectives accurate reflections of reality? Or were they objectives set to please other people? Were you sufficiently aware of the attendees' needs before the meeting?

Was anything missing or forgotten? In the big, expensive meeting I discussed at the beginning of this chapter, we did forget something. We forgot to pay heed to the need for motivation. And because we forgot, the meeting lacked the motivational element that the sales force needed. Because the objectives were wrong, the meeting's flawless tactics didn't produce the desired effects.

Review the original assumptions on which the objectives were based. Was the research accurate? Or were some wrong assumptions made, as in the case when I assumed that an audience didn't need motivation? Possibly your assumptions were entirely subjective rather than based on audience research. That's what happens too much of the time.

Review the basic strategy. Was it really the best way to tackle the meeting or would other possible approaches have been better? Suppose you brought in a speaker whose only purpose was to convince the attendees that the organization was going to grow and develop. How well did it work? If it didn't work, what might you have done instead? Before you even chose that approach you should have had other options.

Finally, review your tactics. Did everybody do their jobs? Did all of the elements of the meeting work? What changes could have been made that would have saved money without diminishing the results? Perhaps the job done by a guest speaker who cost $5,000 could have been done just as well by an audio-visual that would have cost less or by a member of your own organization who would have cost nothing.

Making the Bad News Work for You

You'll always find that a meeting wasn't one hundred percent perfect. If you decide that it was only forty percent as effective as it should have been, you need to establish a remedial program. There's no point in making the same mistakes over and over again.

An ex-Marine who runs meetings for a large financial corporation does his job well with one exception: he runs a talent show in which he actually orders people to come on stage from the audience and perform. The people feel terribly uncomfortable. They don't like it at all.

We did a postmortem with this organizer and pointed out to him that people liked everything except the talent show, which left them feeling negative about the whole meeting. He refused to accept that. People were telling him they liked it. Or at least that's how he interpreted what they were saying. So he keeps doing it and people get a bit more used to it, but it doesn't get any better.

Sometimes there is no obvious bad element. But at the same time there's no clear indication that anything good is coming out of the meeting either. Many people will decide that they can live with a neutral situation. It would be advisable to dig deeper. You might have to fine-tune your targeting and identify people who are refusing to benefit from the meeting.

I did a meeting for the sales staff of a financial company. The objective of the meeting was to motivate them to double their output. From interviews with the salespeople, we knew beforehand that ten of them were resistant to change. They disagreed with the company's ideas on how sales commissions should be structured.

I suggested to the company that these people be left out of the meeting. That suggestion was rejected, and despite the presence of a hostile group, the meeting was full of enthusiasm. The attitude of most of the people was dynamic and aggressive even though the negative element was acting as an anchor, preventing the group as a whole from taking off the way it should have.

After the meeting, it became clear that people who were in direct touch with those who were resisting change weren't doing well. They weren't getting the increased sales that other staff members were enjoying with some popular new services that the company had launched. The company decided to fire the negative group. That action had the effect of opening the floodgates on performance. It immediately improved. Follow-up action to remedy the attitudes of those who had been affected by the fired salespeople was effective.

However, prevention is always better than remedial action. If we had been able to eliminate those negative attitudes before the meeting, we would have had better results.

The more postmortems you do, the better you will get at learning to prevent problems in future meetings. But remember that, like any other skill, identifying and preventing problems takes practice.

It's like playing darts. When you start, you either miss or hit the bulls-eye by pure chance. But by the time you've tossed a few hundred darts, you're on target much of the time. If you do a thorough, honest postmortem after every meeting and apply what you learn to the next meeting, it won't be long before you're hitting the bulls-eye every time.

11

REAPING THE REWARDS

A meeting is inseparable from the organization that holds it. That organization's persona determines the kind of meeting that is held. If the organization has an authoritarian management style, the type in which the top gun talks and everyone else listens, it can have a meeting but it can't have a meeting of minds. If communications in daily business life are in one direction only, they will be in that same direction during the meeting.

Effective meetings are a form of power sharing. Until the last decade or so, effective meetings were a rarity because organizations that believed in power sharing were a rarity. Most executives believed it was their role to make the decisions and their subordinates' role to act on those decisions without asking why. Many hoarded their power, unwilling to share it with the people who worked for them. When they called meetings for their people, it was to put across one message — the organization's message — without reference to the attendees' needs. To make the message as palatable as possible, they would surround it with lots of hoopla and hype, lots of fun and games, and a high decibel level.

Things have changed. Many of today's most successful organizations have learned that participatory management styles are better suited to today's workplace environment than the old-style authoritarian pattern. Power sharing works because it results in better motivation from the top down through an organization and also results in better products and programs.

In the context of meetings, power sharing requires audience research to find out what the attendees want and need. It means designing a meeting to deal with real issues in an open, honest fashion. And it means following up on what the meeting started, because only in the delivery of the promises made at the meeting does power sharing become a reality.

Ten Steps To Successful Meetings

The following ten steps to successful meetings summarize what I've written in this book.

1. Understand your audience. Find out what it needs to know and what it wants to know.
2. Define a *real* objective for your meeting. A real objective is one that is quantifiable. You can perform measurements after the meeting to find out if that objective was achieved.

   Choosing a real, rather than a vague, objective for your meeting is difficult because it requires being honest with yourself and recognizing that some objectives are not achievable because of the nature of your organization, your people, or your industry. If your sales force has been turned off by inflexible management attitudes, for example, motivating that sales force may not be an attainable meeting objective.
3. Design your meeting based on a strategy that solves a problem, keeping in mind that a meeting is an opportunity to build on your organization's strategic objectives. The problem your meeting addresses should have been defined by your objectives. If, for example, your objective is to raise the profile of your charitable organization in various regions across the country, then your problem is to find ways to do that.
4. Plan your meeting the way a theater director would mount a play. Make it one large communications project. Most people plan meetings the way they would plan a picnic in the country. They worry more about getting there and about the food than about whether it's going to be a good picnic or a bad picnic. But if the picnic site is infested with ants, or if people get bored after they've eaten and there's nothing else to do, or if it rains and there's nowhere else to go, it won't be a good picnic.

   A theater director looks at the overall impact that the production will have on the audience. He or she sees it as a communications event that will impart a certain message or a certain feeling to the audience, and the director works on all of the details with that goal in mind.

5. The meeting should follow an action plan that organizes the meeting preparations over a period of months. Identify what has to be done, when it has to be done, and by whom it has to be done. The action plan identifies the responsibilities of every member of the meeting team as well as what can be delegated to others.

6. Do not be seduced by high technology or gimmicks. What you have to say is more important than the way you say it. If you don't have anything important to say, or the meagerness of your message has to be masked by gimmickry, then don't hold a meeting. Or hold a smaller meeting that's been advertised in advance as dealing with only one issue.

7. Each facet of the meeting should be treated with attention and care. If a building contains too many cracked bricks, the entire building may be in jeopardy even if most of the bricks are solid. Just because the audio-visual equipment is in perfect shape, the registration table has been set up in a highly professional manner, and the banquet is sure to draw raves, that doesn't guarantee a successful event.

   Other details may have been neglected that could spell disaster. Will the keynote speaker really deliver what is required? Has he or she been briefed on the nature of the audience and the objective of the meeting? An ill-prepared speaker is sure to do more harm than good.

   Perhaps certain people are going to be playing key roles in the meeting and need training in their presentation skills. Some of them are resisting this training. Someone has to sit down with them and deal with the problem.

   Remember that one negative in a meeting isn't cancelled out by one positive. Instead, that one negative will cancel out a dozen positives. People remember what went wrong; they usually don't notice what goes smoothly.

8. As the meeting coordinator pursues each detail, he or she must remember that the aim is to create one overall impact. The meeting is a mountain, not a series of little hills. Everything that is done must be related in some way to the basic objective established by the executive director.

9. Ensure that follow-up is carried out after the meeting on the most important aspects. Follow-up is the most neglected element in meeting planning. It is also the most important element in ensuring successful results. Note, however, that I am suggesting follow-up on the "important aspects." If somebody didn't like a drink he was served and he wants you to send a nasty letter to the hotel, you can ignore him. One drink is not important. Of course, if there were major problems with suppliers, these would have to be handled. But it's more important to follow up with the meeting attendees, to ensure that the improvements in morale, creativity, knowledge, and skill that everyone worked so hard to achieve are maintained as the meeting recedes into history.

10. Learn from the mistakes. It's through coping with problems and analyzing mistakes that we grow and improve.

The Future of Meetings

A new type of executive is replacing the authoritarian decision makers who used to run many of our organizations. These new executives rely more on creativity and a sense of gamesmanship. They have a much greater understanding than did their predecessors in the executive suites of the importance of motivation and teamwork, in leading a group of diverse individuals toward a single goal.

That difference is significant, and we see it reflected in meetings that are becoming more and more people-oriented as opposed to thing-oriented. The focus is increasingly on the attendees rather than on technology or products or statistics.

New technology is increasing the effectiveness of communications while challenging the creative ability of the people who originate the messages. That's because more effective media tend to show up irrelevant or empty content. Interactive video technology, for example, gives the attendees a choice of responses. They become actively involved in the material rather than just consuming it passively as happens with more common technology such as films or slide shows.

These messages had better be convincing and viable. If they're not, the audience will immediately be aware of the fact. If the organization hasn't thought the issues through, that will become apparent. If it is trying to hide something, that fact may be quickly exposed.

More advanced technology will force meetings to be much more relevant than in the past to the needs of the people who do the work of the organization or make up the membership of the organization. If meetings lack that relevance, audiences will dismiss them as boring.

Costs will continue to rise. As a result, meeting design will become more important than ever. Planners will no longer be able to get away with simply "putting a meeting on." They are going to have to show real returns on the company's investment.

Some recent concepts in meetings will become increasingly popular. One is the traveling road show, in which about a dozen people take a meeting on the road into the different regions in which an organization operates. Traveling meetings are more efficient because they are less costly and less time-consuming. The downside is that they aren't necessarily as productive as big meetings because opportunities for networking are lost, as is the crowd effect that gives a sense of importance to the individual and to the event itself. The crowd makes one feel part of a larger whole and plays an important part in motivating individuals.

The traveling road-show concept will advance to such a point that some meetings will take place entirely on tape. The tape will be sent out from head office along with some experts, and the local senior executive will hold his or her own workshops and seminars to follow up the information on the tape.

Meetings will become much more interactive because that is what attendees are demanding. Audiences will interact much more with what is happening on the screen or stage, through computers, workshops, and open sessions.

The tie-in between incentives and meetings will become closer. There is increasing demand for incentives with meetings attached. For example, a group of people, winners of a travel incentive, will be brought to a location. There, a meeting will be held to congratulate them, train them, and motivate them, after which they will be left to enjoy their vacation.

The treatment of meeting follow-up will become increasingly sophisticated. In an earlier chapter, I discussed a company that planned a series of three linked meetings over a three-year span.

That sort of thing will become commonplace as more organizations adopt a long-term, strategic approach as a way of getting the most out of the money they spend on internal communications.

The "Big Results" Ingredient

Power sharing doesn't come naturally. The more power one has, the less vulnerable one feels. Therefore, to share power requires a great deal of courage. It requires belief in yourself and in the individuals with whom you are sharing power.

Companies are political entities as are service clubs and other organizations that hold meetings. Sharing power implies giving up power and in a political world that is a very hard thing to do. But the rewards are tremendous.

When you learn to share power in a meeting, your biggest reward is in the feedback you get from the audience. Having their share of power encourages people to get involved, to generate ideas, to work harder, to cooperate, to take risks. On the other hand, being powerless strips them of motivation. They become stubborn as mules. An organization that refuses to share power deprives itself of the energy, commitment, and brilliance of its people.

The truism that the whole is greater than the sum of the parts is particularly applicable in the context of meetings. I recall sitting in Winchester Cathedral, admiring the craftmanship of the workers who built it. The cathedral is built of thousands of bricks, and while the bricks are perfectly fitted together, not one brick looks like a cathedral.

Each tiny element is indistinguishable from the next. The same is true of a meeting. One small section of one audio-visual presentation isn't particularly important or significant in itself. But it's one brick and it has to fit into an overall design. Like a cathedral, a meeting must have an architect who understands how each little piece fits together and why.

You must have a grand design in which the whole is greater than the sum of the parts. And you must be committed to sharing power with your audience. That's how I've been successful at designing meetings, and that's how you can be successful too. But I wouldn't be honest if I didn't admit that it's the most difficult approach you can take.

It's much easier to ignore hard realities when staging a meeting. It's easier to fool yourself into thinking you're dealing with real issues when you're not, to fool yourself into thinking that your audience should not know about the important issues in your organization.

The old-fashioned, unilateral meeting style gets a result. People will probably get the message and they may even have a good time. But only the power-sharing meeting gets significant results — results that lead to growth in the people attending the meeting and in the organization for which they work. Those are the only kind of results that count — big results.

SUGGESTED READINGS

General

Coleman, Finkel. *Professional Guide to Successful Meetings.* Boston: Herman Publishing, 1976.

Kulhanek, Joan. "Guess Who's Coming to Dinner." Toronto: CAE Magazine, May 1985.

Nadler, Leonard and Zeace Nadler. *The Conference Book: How to Successfully Design, Plan, Staff and Run Conferences of 25 or More People.* Houston: Gulf Publishing, 1977.

Prince, George M. *The Practice of Creativity.* New York: Collier, 1972.

Executive

Auger, B. Y. *How to Run Better Business Meetings: An Executive Guide to Meetings that Get Things Done.* St. Paul, Minn.: 3M Company, 1979.

Interaction Associates: Strategy Notebook. San Francisco: Interaction Associates, 1972.

Jefferies, James R. and Jefferson D. Bates. *The Executive's Guide to Meetings, Conferences and AV Presentations.* New York: McGraw-Hill, 1983.

Secretan, Lance. *Managerial Moxie.* Toronto: Gage Publishing, 1985.

Communications

Curtis, Dan B. *Communications for Problem-Solving.* New York: Wiley, 1979.

Rothwell, Dan J. and James I. Costigan. *Interpersonal Communications.* Columbus, Ohio: Charles E. Merrill, 1975.

Thompson, James J. *Instructional Communications.* New York: American Book Company, 1969.

Planning Process

Drain, Robert H. *Successful Conference and Convention Planning.* New York: McGraw-Hill, 1978.

Favreau, Donald F. *Planning and Conducting Successful Meetings and Conferences.* Albany, N.Y.: Lane Press, 1970.

Hegarty, Edward J. *How to Run Better Meetings.* New York: McGraw-Hill, 1975.

Tropman, John E. *Effective Meetings.* Beverly Hills, Calif.: University of Michigan School of Social Work, 1980.

Workshops and Seminars

Madsen, Paul O. *The Person Who Chairs the Meeting.* Valley Forge, Penn.: Judson Press, 1973.

Maier, Norman, R. F. *Problem-Solving Discussions and Conferences.* New York: McGraw-Hill, 1963.

Newstrom, John W. and Edward Scannell. *Games Trainers Play: Experimental Learning Exercise.* New York: McGraw-Hill, 1980.

Meeting Design

Berbe, Eric. *The Structure and Dynamics of Organizations and Groups.* New York: Grove Press, 1966.

Delbecq, Andre L., Andrew H. Van De Ven and David H. Gustafson. *Group Techniques and Delphi Processes.* La Jolla, Calif.: N.T.L. Learning Resources Corp., 1975.

Homme, Lloyd. *A Behavioural Technology Exists: Here and Now.* Oaklawn, Ill.: Westinghouse Learning Corporation, 1970.

Johnson, David W. and Frank P. Johnson. *Joining Together: Group Theory and Group Skills.* Englewood Cliffs, N.J.: Prentice-Hall, 1975.

Schindler-Rainman, Eva and Ronald Lippitt. *Taking Your Meetings out of the Doldrums.* San Diego, Calif.: University Associates, 1975.

This, Leslie E. *The Small Meeting Planner.* Houston: Gulf Publishing, 1979.

INDEX

DATE DUE